RAISA

RAISA

Urda Jürgens

Translated from the German by
Sylvia Clayton

WEIDENFELD AND NICOLSON

LONDON

First published in Great Britain in 1990 by
George Weidenfeld & Nicolson Limited
91 Clapham High Street
London SW4 7TA

ISBN 0 297 81102 9

Printed in Great Britain by Butler and Tanner Ltd,
Frome and London

Copyright © 1990 by ECON Verlag GmbH,
Dusseldorf, Vienna and New York

Translation copyright © 1990 by Sylvia Clayton

All photographs reproduced by courtesy of ECON
Verlag and Jürgens/Ost & Europa Photo

British Library Cataloguing in Publication Data
applied for

Published in Germany in 1990 by ECON Verlag
GmbH

Contents

Foreword

Raisa Gorbachev, the railwayman's daughter who became first Lady of the Soviet Union, was not born under a lucky star. She has had to work with intelligence, composure, energy and discipline to make her way in life, from a railway wagon home to the presidential dacha.

When I saw her self-assured yet reserved charm during her travels abroad with her husband, I was immensely curious about this unknown Raisa, who appeared to shoot comet-like across the media landscape of the world, in sharp contrast to the scarcely known wives of former heads of the Kremlin. I determined to pursue this new star in the media firmament and my encounters with Raisa herself encouraged me in my quest.

I found I had given myself a difficult assignment. There were many obstacles to overcome, but I let nothing distract me from my obsession with Raisa, even though I quickly discovered that *glasnost* and *perestroika* end where the Soviet First Family begins. It was precisely the fact that I was exploring exciting, largely unknown territory that drove me on.

My work eventually crystallized into a fascinating portrait of a woman in world politics, a woman who has never been content simply to smooth her husband's path, an emancipated woman in whom ambition, joy and the desire to be useful combine with intelligence and feminine persuasiveness. They are qualities that can be seen in a Soviet leader's wife for the first time in Russian history.

1

The Railway Child

Raya was the pet name her parents gave to their eldest child. Her birth is registered in the town records of Vessolayarsk on 5 January 1932, under the name of Raisa Maximovna Titorenko, daughter of Maxim Titorenko, railway worker and his wife, Shura Paradina. The Russians, far more than other people, like to use diminutives instead of full names: Maria becomes Maya or Marushka, Mikhail turns into Misha, Raisa into Raya. The name recorded on the birth certificate is generally used only when the person concerned is in some kind of trouble. People can go through life without ever being called by their actual first name.

The father and mother of Shura Paradina, Raya's grandparents, kept a small shop in Vessolayarsk. Everything that could be bought in Soviet Russia at that time was on sale there. It wasn't much, but it provided a meagre living for the family.

Shura was eighteen when she met Maxim, a railway worker eight years her senior, who came from Tishemilov in the Ukraine. They met in Vessolayarsk, a town of about 8000 people. He had previously been employed at the little railway station of Lokot, building freight trains for the town of Ridder, now known as Leninogorsk. He liked Shura, a cheerful, resolute, vivacious girl. They felt they could look forward to a lifetime together. Maxim and Shura were married amid tears and vows and promises of lifelong commitment. Their wedding had nothing showy or ostentatious about it. Why should it be grand? There was love and trust, and also confidence.

Soon a child was on the way. The Titorenkos looked forward

to the birth with joy, but also with some anxiety, for there was no hospital in Vessolayarsk, and no midwife. Maxim, like all expectant fathers, was understandably nervous. He didn't want to take any chances. It was a cold January with deep snow. A child was going to come into the world, but when?

Rubtsovsk, the nearest town, which offered a hospital and professional care, was some thirty kilometres away. Maxim drove his young wife to Rubtsovsk in a horse and trap. Shura was probably warmly wrapped in blankets, but thirty kilometres through icy cold in a horse-drawn vehicle in the ninth month of pregnancy could scarcely be regarded as a comfortable journey.

The people of this part of the Soviet Union are not accustomed to mollycoddling. Everyday life and the nature of the terrain itself has made them tough. The child brought happiness to the Titorenkos. Little Raisa was born brown-eyed, healthy and active, with reddish-brown hair, which, incidentally, she would as a young girl twist into eye-catching copper-coloured plaits, worn crossed over her head for dances. However, she always obediently allowed her brother to escort her home.

Baby Raisa and her mother came back from hospital to Vessolayarsk, healthy and content. Shura was then about nineteen years old. The winter of 1932 was exceptionally severe, but Raya grew sturdily through her first year, confirming the Russian folk belief that the healthiest children are those who have to battle through hard weather in their earliest months of life.

On the broad plains of the region the level of the sky seems to change every day. Sometimes the flat roofs of the low wooden houses appear almost to touch the clouds; on other days the high blue sky accentuates the modest scale of the dwellings.

Vessolayarsk, which might be described as Raisa's home town, is an unlovely little spot in the Altai mountain range that divides Europe from Asia. It is less than a thousand kilometres from Vessolayarsk to the borders of China and Mongolia. People speak a mixture of languages, and cultural standards are quite different from those of European Moscow.

Vessolayarsk is located in western Siberia, a name which carries disturbing dual overtones, of nature and death. In Siberia's forests and woods, in its tundra and its never-ending plains, nature can still be found untouched and unspoiled, though today it is of course no longer unexplored.

2

Even at the time of the nineteenth-century tsars, Siberia was considered a deadly country. The Russians described it as 'their biggest prison', and successive rulers of Russia made use of it in that way, Stalin not least. To be sent to Siberia was a sentence of banishment for people who opposed authority in the vast Russian empire. Siberia, the local inhabitants said, was the territory for people without papers, who managed to escape from the bureaucratic and penal clutches of the Communist Party. Siberia, they said, either killed you or liberated you.

Little Raisa lived in Vessolayarsk for two winters and two summers. Her father put in long hours and he was often away, but his position as a railway worker brought with it a few privileges that other jobs did not. In an enormous country like Russia rail transport played an obviously important role. There was no other way in which the huge distances could be covered. Today the railways remain the arteries of the USSR. Any serious blockage of the arteries restricts the circulation of the blood, with catastrophic results. If the railway link breaks, the whole of Soviet society is in jeopardy.

The Soviets were conscious of this from the outset, and the social status of the railway worker's job was correspondingly upgraded. The railway engineer was a man to be respected among the intelligentsia; railwaymen formed a privileged brigade among the working class. They enjoyed an above average salary, and they were among the first Russian workers to be entitled to an annual holiday. They followed the civil servants as the second group to receive a retirement pension. Their job also freed them from the wearisome search for clothing – they had their uniform, which in itself put them in a different class. In addition, the state put at the disposal of the railway workers simple little wooden houses, which, if they had no modern comforts, at least provided a roof over people's heads.

The Titorenko family enjoyed these amenities and counted themselves members of the privileged section of the provincial working class. On the debit side, they had to contend with the real disadvantages of the job. Maxim, the father, had to work where he was sent. The railway system was at bottom, even under the tsars, a matter of strategic importance to the country, and railway workers, even in peacetime, had to respond to military planning and objectives. The army's demands were paramount.

3

Railway families had, as a result, some material comfort, but at the price of an unsettled existence.

In 1934, when Raisa was two, her brother Yevgeny was born, and that year the Titorenko family had to move. Maxim was posted to Chernigov in the Ukraine, which was not like moving to the next village or driving thirty kilometres in the pony and trap to Rubtsovsk. The family had to travel some 3000 kilometres from Vessolayarsk, a journey that separated the children from their grandparents and Raisa's mother from her own mother. It must have been a painful parting. The old people were left behind and the young ones journeyed into the future.

For the Titorenkos moving to the Ukraine meant a considerable upheaval. Shura, who despite the arrival of her two children, had not given up her job as a railway inspector, lost the help of the grandparents in looking after them. At that time Maxim was earning between 750 and 800 roubles a month, which sounds quite a reasonable wage, and for the 1930s was not bad pay. The money would today be worth between 35 and 40 roubles, enough to keep the family at subsistence level, enabling them to buy the basic necessities of life with perhaps an occasional bottle of vodka. Things cost less in the 1930s than they do today, but the Titorenkos had two children and their resources were severely limited. Shura simply had to continue working, and, like so many women, divided her energies between her job and her family.

Then came disaster, and years of enforced silence, hopelessness and daily anxiety in the Titorenko family: the far-reaching hand of Stalinism found them. In 1935 Maxim Titorenko was arrested and imprisoned in one of the network of labour camps that Stalin had established across the country. Imprisonment spread over the nation unobtrusively, in waves. There were show trials. The OGPU, the Soviet secret police, arrested not only everybody who criticized the totalitarian regime, but also those who were merely suspected of dissenting from official opinion. In the mid-Thirties there were some 16 million people in Stalin's camps. Innocent people, who died there; brave people who cared about their country and spoke out.

Maxim Titorenko's offence was that he had spoken critically among his fellow workmen about the dreadful incidents and consequences that had resulted from the collectivization of the land. He was held in custody until 1939, when he left the

4

Solovetski labour camp weakened in health and returned to his wife and children. He had survived. He was one of the few.

During Maxim's years of imprisonment things were not as dire as they could have been for Shura and the children. Unlike the dependent families of some prisoners, the Titorenkos were not simply turned out into the street. Shura and her two children, Raisa and Yevgeny were deprived of their home, but given a railway wagon in which to live. It was a goods wagon of the most primitive design, but it did provide them with 8 or 10 square yards of living space. Raisa's mother divided the wagon into three sections. The stove stood by the door, and was used for heating and cooking. One-third of the wagon became the kitchen and living room, one-third the bedroom, and the other third the lavatory. There was no electric light, just candles, and water had to be fetched from the well. But there was one advantage. Shura was able to work, providing basic subsistence for the family.

Raisa's earliest childhood years were spent not just in anxiety and insecurity but in actual poverty. She had her jobs to do. While her mother was at work, she had to look after her younger brother and do some of the cleaning. Raisa was a real help to her mother at that time, according to her best friend Lydia Budyka. Her childhood memories are not the traditional ones.

Her mother bore the heaviest burden, often weeping over the injustice and loneliness of her situation. In the circumstances, it would have been especially useful to have grandparents on the spot. It was not, however, simply a matter of being thousands of kilometres apart; travel was prohibited. Exceptions were made only at the highest level. Shura, Raisa and Yevgeny had to fend for themselves.

Raisa still remembers how much strength, energy and care her mother concentrated on her children, how she cooked for them and struggled to give them a sense of security and well-being, so that the harsh regime imposed by their situation would not destroy their confidence.

'She made us clothes, she cooked, she sang little songs, she was there, and we felt protected,' Raisa Gorbachev has said about those years. 'We used to go mushrooming, collecting them and drying them. Our mother really watched over us and insisted on a certain amount of discipline, which was soon of value to us.'

Her close relationship with her mother developed certain traits in Raisa's own character. Raisa, like her mother, is today very concerned about the welfare of her own family, and she shows the same sense of duty that her mother demonstrated so admirably. She is a good housewife, though her opportunities to prove this have been limited, because of the duties her status as the wife of Mikhail Gorbachev entail. For many years the wife of the head of the Kremlin did her own housework, cooking and shopping. Up until 1985, when Mikhail Gorbachev became General Secretary, she insisted on her right to perform certain domestic tasks herself, for instance to put home-cooked meals and home-baked food on the Gorbachev table. She tried to distance her family from problems, as her mother had done. Her entire idea of family life revolves around peace and harmony. Her temperament and her single-mindedness Raisa inherited from her resolute mother.

Her friend Lydia Budyka says: 'Raisa is very like her mother. Her mother is intelligent and full of energy. Although she is not a highly educated person, she is extremely perceptive. Her father was a shy man, quiet, friendly and very tender-hearted. Raisa was greatly attached to her father. She often wept for him when he was in the prison camp. In appearance Raisa resembles neither her father nor her mother.'

For many years Ivan Dimitrievich Pocheriv, a retired teacher, has been collecting material for a history of Vessolayarsk. In fact, as recently as 1988 there was an old woman living there, almost a hundred years old, who could remember Raisa's mother as an 'agile, sharp-witted girl', qualities Raisa herself possesses. Pocheriv wrote to Raisa Gorbachev asking her some questions about her birthplace. She replied promptly, confirming that Vessolayarsk was her place of birth and expressing regret that so far circumstances had not permitted her to return there. Her letter now reposes in the archives of the Vessolayarsk party committee.

In 1939 her father, as I have said, was released from the prison camp. He came back physically weak, but not broken in spirit. His heart and his body were marked by his suffering in the camp, where he had found friends, among them Dmitri Sergeyevich Likhachev, the prisoner who had the next plank bed. At night they secretly exchanged words of comfort and talked about their fears for the fate of their country.

Likhachev had protested against the destruction of Russian culture under Stalin, against the neglect of artistic monuments and the squandering of Russia's cultural resources. Before he was sent to the camp he had fiercely criticized the public irresponsibility he found everywhere.

In the labour camp he talked about all this to Maxim Titorenko. The railway worker learned of the artistic wealth that Russia possessed in spite of her material poverty. He also became conscious of the way art and culture could enrich the life of an individual and of society. Raisa's father was discharged from the camp in some ways better educated than when he entered it. Half a century later, that same Dmitri Likhachev became one of the founders of the Soviet government's Cultural Foundation, and Raisa, the daughter of his fellow prisoner Titorenko and the wife of Mikhail Gorbachev, the General Secretary, would co-operate with him in the task of encouraging and conserving art and culture in Gorbachev's Russia.

The beginning of Raisa's school days in 1939 coincided with her father's return from the labour camp, as it did with the outbreak of the Second World War. At the time of the German advance into Poland, few people in the USSR regarded this as a threat of aggression against the Soviet Union, interpreting the Hitler–Stalin pact as promising peace to Russia.

However, by the autumn of 1939 a massive resettlement of major Soviet industries in the interior of the USSR had been initiated, and giant armament factories were set up in the Urals. Whole establishments were transferred to the Urals from the west. One train after another rumbled out of the Ukraine and western Russia, bound for new production centres in Siberia.

The policy of shipping industries wholesale across a continent involved the Titorenkos, as a 'railway family', in frequent moves. They had to make their home wherever Maxim Titorenko was posted by the railway management, and so the children were always changing school. In those years, Raisa's school books began to read like a series of halts on the rail map of the Soviet Union. Educational continuity was not in itself too big a problem, since at that time all the schools in the USSR conformed to the same curriculum. But the children were constantly having to get used to new classes, friends and teachers. The itinerant life of the Titorenkos may be one reason why the young Raisa was thought to be so reserved. She seldom had the chance to get used to new surroundings before moving on. It was rare for railway families, chased from post to post across the country, to be provided with decent accommodation. They had to improvise, often living as families in railway wagons, which were then simply hitched to the locomotive to take them to their next destination.

While Raisa Titorenko was attending school in a succession of towns and villages, a peasant boy, ten months older than she, was working with his father on the land at Privolnoye, a place so small as to be hardly visible on an Ordnance Survey map of southern Russia. Some three thousand people lived in the district of Privolnoye, in remote country villages. The nearest town was several hours' walk away, and it was a day's journey to get to Stavropol, the regional capital. The boy was called Mikhail, eldest son of Sergei Gorbachev, an agricultural worker.

Mikhail – Misha to his family – was leading a life not so different from that of other boys of his age. His carefree childhood was short. He soon had to help his father on the farm as well as do his lessons. The days were long, and the only difference the school holidays made was that the whole of his day was then spent in the fields.

Village life makes a deeper impression on people than urban life. Family relationships are often closer, while working together every day strengthens a sense of mutual reliance. Grandparents often help with bringing up the children. Sharing tasks is a necessity. Extended families have different standards from nuclear families. So there is nothing unusual about the fact that Misha's grandparents feature prominently in his memories. With his father Sergei serving as a soldier in the war and his mother obliged to work away from Privolnoye, his grandparents were left to bring up Misha themselves. If Raisa grew up as a mother's child, he grew up as a grandparents' child.

The personality of a man is shaped not just by his upbringing but by other external factors. One of these is the countryside in which he grows up, the place where he always feels at home. The region around Stavropol, where Mikhail Gorbachev was born, had existed historically on the frontiers of Russian imperialism. Cossacks, who were free farmers, owing allegiance to no feudal lord, settled the rich, fertile land, which could not only feed its owners, but enabled them to grow surplus produce for sale.

The Cossacks lived better than the serfs in other regions, but not infrequently they had to defend their freedom by the sword. The nomads of the steppes regularly attacked the much coveted land around Stavropol. The long tradition of independence produced, as one might expect, proud men, who liked to decide their own fate without regard to the authorities. Such factors influence people permanently, even when conditions change. Officials sent by the state to organize collectivization in Cossack regions at the end of the 1920s and the beginning of the 1930s found they had a rugged job on their hands. Surrendering property meant serfdom. Quite a few Cossacks opposed the surrender, and, as was the custom of the region, opposed it by force of arms.

Conditions in the Altai Mountains of Raisa Gorbachev's homeland were, in spite of the great geographical distance between them, similar to those in her husband's region. On either side of the mountain range stretched broad plains, making them a world of their own. The areas around Stavropol and in the Altai Mountains were called 'territories', not without reason. They were territories in which at that time a number of organizations politically and geographically linked with Europe were to be found.

The Altai region was used as a place of refuge by adventurous Russians, who travelled individually and in groups thousands of miles from their place of birth in order to live in freedom. They found sanctuary in the Altai from army officials, tax inspectors or bailiffs. They lived on the products of their own labour. Those who chose could join a large community of free men, in which each had the right to personal development. Neighbours were no problem. Doors and gates to the wooden houses in the villages were left unlocked. Members of the Russian Orthodox Church, who had also settled in the Altai region, did not try to impose their religion on anyone. People lived together in harmony. Times were often hard, but this did not cause divisions in a community which had learnt that unity was the key to survival. The sole possession of many people was this harmonious communal life, but it counted for much with them.

Neither the Cossack villages of southern Russia nor those of the Altai Mountains were unaffected by the new Soviet regime, but much remained as it had been in the past. People wanted the past preserved. They resisted innovation. Entering school thus meant entering a wider world. Every day you learned something new. The way to school was in the truest sense the way to life.

School work could not be the children's only daily task; household duties and jobs for other people in the village often took up more time than actual lessons, but in school both Mikhail, the peasant boy, and Raisa, the railwayman's daughter, displayed a genuine eagerness for knowledge. That is, of course, nothing unusual in itself. History is full of examples of children from poor homes who put more effort into gaining education than children born with greater material advantages. Both Mikhail and Raisa studied with unflagging enthusiasm throughout their school days.

But back to Raisa. Her school days began with the compulsory four-grade primary school. At that time the age for starting school was legally fixed at seven only in the towns and workers' settlements of the Soviet Union. It was not until 1949 that this was enforced by statute throughout the country. In the first two school years boys and girls were educated together; after that they were taught separately. Raisa had more than thirty fellow pupils at her primary school. Until the fourth grade they were taught all subjects by the same teacher.

The timetable for the first year was fairly simple: an hour each of physical education, drawing and singing, and a few hours of mathematics; all the rest of the time was devoted to the Russian language and a first acquaintance with literature. A new world opened up for the child; she learned to read. Again it was her mother who encouraged her. Shura believed that reading was one of the most important things in life. Learning to read was a character-building process. She had no difficulty in making Raisa exert herself, when things didn't come easily.

In 1940 Raisa's younger sister Ludmilla was born. This entailed more work. Raisa, along with Yevgeny, had to help her mother, now in a full-time job, to look after the baby. The parents divided their time, as far as they could, between their work and their family. It was probably the children who lost out.

Raisa had only been at school for two years – she had not yet completed her primary education – when Germany attacked the Soviet Union and war began for the Russian people. Again, a comprehensive industrial relocation programme was launched, embracing entire industries situated in the Russian heartlands. Resources in the west of the country had to be repositioned, put into production and turned over to defence requirements. The

10

only means of transporting factory equipment was by rail. The railwaymen came under military orders.

'Everything for the Front' was the bugle call slogan Stalin sounded to call his country to arms. Stalin's illusions about his pact with Hitler had vanished in a giant puff of smoke, the smoke of burning Russian houses, towns and villages. The people of the USSR made unbelievable sacrifices for Stalin in the Great Patriotic War against Nazi Germany.

For Raisa and her family this meant another period of living on the railway. Life was governed by random emergency arrangements. The possessions of the Titorenko family were greatly reduced, and they were driven to the point of physical exhaustion. Certainly Russian children received preferential treatment. Outside the combat zones schooling continued relatively normally. The children, however, did contribute directly to the war effort by working in shifts in armaments factories and on the land, collecting scrap iron, caring for the elderly and their own younger brothers and sisters.

Raisa was a second mother to Evgeny and Ludmilla. Recalling the war years she stresses: 'Mama Shura [she calls her mother by that name to this day] always tried, despite the pressures of the war, to care for her children and protect them.' Although Raisa did not have to cope with the immediate experiences of the battlefront – pain, hunger and death – she and her family led a disrupted existence. She encountered different schools and different teachers constantly. Had she any friends at this period of her life?

Children need friends in order to develop as people, and it must inevitably have been very lonely for Raisa in the frenetic wartime atmosphere. Often she had to face curious looks from fellow pupils who were, of course, strangers to her, and she must have wished for a close friend, the kind of friend one reads about in books.

Raisa was a reserved girl, who did her lessons well and enjoyed reading more than many children her age, which may in small measure have protected her against the harsher realities of her life. Through her books she could dream and escape into another world. In the real world the war continued relentlessly and her duties cut across her dreams, shattering the bridge between dream and reality. Children regard life differently from the way adults imagine they do. Undoubtedly there were times of enjoyment and gaiety, from which the children could draw the strength and energy that enables them to survive adversity.

Like all Russian children, Raisa was enthusiastic about her political education. She wore the red scarf of the Young Pioneers, and like all pupils from the third to the seventh grade, she could recite its motto by heart.

> When you put on your Pioneer scarf
> You must guard it.
> It has the same red colour
> As our country's flag.

Children throughout the Soviet Union wore the scarf with its motto: 'Thank you, Comrade Stalin, for a happy childhood.'

Every morning Raisa, like all the other children, had to repeat the Young Pioneer greeting: 'On with the struggle for the cause of Lenin and Stalin, be ready. Always ready.'

She could not have known that a ministerial decree published in 1943 spoke of bringing the Young Pioneers into a more committed relationship with the Soviet people and the Bolshevik party and of fomenting passionate hatred of the enemies of the people. The Young Pioneers, a children's organization named after Lenin, had become in Stalin's mind a children's political party, led by the state youth organization. The Young Pioneers' scarf was worn with pride and handled as reverently as the Communist party card.

Raisa was the embodiment of the declared aims of the Young Pioneers, having a positive attitude towards work and learning, demonstrating diligence, endurance, punctuality, courage and physical fitness. She grew up in this Stalin-dominated atmosphere. Whether she was impervious to it, how far she was affected by it, who can judge today? How much do we know about the inner life of children?

In 1943, having passed through primary school, Raisa began to attend middle school, at the end of which came the possibility of further college education. The timetable broadened to accommodate such subjects as history, geography, botany, zoology, the study of the constitution, foreign languages and in the final year, psychology.

12

A course on psychology may seem a strange item in the syllabus, given the degree of Stalinist suppression of free thought in the USSR at the time, a restriction totally at variance with the principles of psychology. It is hard to imagine a more violent contradiction, but Raisa, brought up under a system founded on contradictions, was not conscious of it. She was imprisoned, entangled in the Stalinist web.

The effect of her father's prison experience and her mother's constant drive to push Raisa to high achievement can be understood more easily. The Stalin period was a time of secret, deadly threats. Maxim Titorenko and his wife had experienced this at first hand. They had become quietist. Under Stalin, to be unobtrusive was the way to survive.

At middle school Raisa had about thirty-three hours of instruction per week. The school regime was strict and left little scope for the creative development of the child's personality. There had been reformers who had recognized this as educationally disastrous, but they were defeated by the mistrust, the destructive will of a proliferating party bureaucracy, which was growing steadily stronger. It was a school that demanded total obedience, total discipline; it was fully expressive of Stalin's ruthless ideology. But there was no alternative. There was no comparison with other educational systems. The USSR was oppressed in every aspect of its existence, including the education and upbringing of its children.

The Soviet school year was divided into four terms. At the end of each term pupils were given marks for all subjects and a special mark for behaviour. Girls all had to wear uniforms, hairstyles had to be simple and cosmetics were banned.

Raisa remembers that in her school textbooks the pictures of all the 'revolutionaries' who had suffered under Stalin were either made unrecognizable with ink marks, or cut out altogether. Sometimes the eyes of the 'revolutionaries' were pierced with scissors. Wartime pupils had to share one book between four, since there were not enough to go around. Children were accordingly allowed to study in groups, and discovered early in life how to learn collectively.

Raisa had to assimilate the immense mass of information that children were required to absorb. Examinations in Soviet schools were regular and tough. It was a doctrinaire school system that pressurized children to become achievers. Superb natural teachers can, as we all know, make a doctrinaire system tolerable, but even they would not have been able to alter it. Raisa did learn. She was a quiet, conscientious student. It came instinctively to her to do homework properly, to perform efficiently, even excellently at school. She was motivated by thoughts of her country, of Stalin, and perhaps also of what her parents might say. Stalin was everywhere. Wherever she looked – in the classroom, on the wall newspapers, on the hoardings in every street – Stalin was there. Stalin was present in people's minds, as a respected prophet or a terrifying dictator; he had a godlike power. In every essay she wrote Raisa had to praise Stalin. The more glowing the praise, the higher the mark. In Stalin's name untold suffering was inflicted on people, and in his name men struggled, education was provided and children learned their lessons.

In 1945, when Raisa was thirteen, the war ended. Russia was devastated. The railways were once again of supreme importance in the rebuilding of the country.

A new era began, which for Raisa was a return to an itinerant way of life. Coping with post-war conditions demanded the energy, courage and ingenuity of every single Russian. It is possible that Raisa had to divide her time even more drastically than before between household chores, caring for her younger brother and sister and doing her schoolwork. Yet it seems certain that her mother tried as far as possible to give her ambitious, talented daughter scope for taking advantage of the educational opportunities open to her. Raisa was going to have a better chance in life than Shura Paradina, the resourceful girl from the village in western Siberia, had enjoyed.

Raisa's horizons were still limited. Signs of hope, however, began to appear. If pupils were diligent, if they conformed politically and made use of their talents and intelligence, they had a reasonable chance of succeeding.

'At school Raisa was keen on group projects. She played an active part in school life, being a natural leader even then,' says her friend Lydia.

Raisa did not disappoint her mother. She finished school with the highest marks and a gold medal. In the tenth grade she was given a '5', the top mark, for every subject, and passed all her

exams with distinction. Her favourite subjects were history, literature and the humanities.

Her future husband, Mikhail Gorbachev, received only a silver
medal. In German he didn't reach the 'Very Good' standard.
Only one in a hundred Soviet school leavers was awarded a gold
medal, one in fifty a silver. School standards were strict; exact
knowledge was required. All school leavers who gained a gold or
silver medal qualified automatically for entrance to one of the
colleges or universities of the USSR.

The end of her school career was for Raisa the beginning of a
new, far more stable existence. She was accepted as a student at
Moscow State University. At her obligatory interview with the
Dean, Raisa revealed herself as a conscientious student and a
genuine fighter for Communism.

At first the life of Raisa's parents went on as before. It was not
until the beginning of the 1970s that things eased up for Shura
and Maxim. The railway brought them to Krasnodar, a town
only a few kilometres from Stavropol – a place which was to have
a special meaning for the Titorenkos when their daughter settled
there as Raisa Gorbachev. At this time these events were in the
future. We must retrace our steps to the years when Raisa went
off to Moscow; when, like a bird she left the nest, as the Russians
say.

2

Moscow Student Days

Agroup photograph taken in 1954 at the end of the academic year consists of 132 portraits: twenty-two members of staff in rectangular insets and 110 students in oval-shaped ones. Young faces and older faces, curiosity and experience, zest for living and melancholy, initiative and resignation. The individual stories and the collective history of an entire nation can be deduced from the restricted sample of people in the photograph, the student intake of the Philosophy Faculty of Moscow State University, who were thrown together by chance in 1949 and five years later in 1954 were sent out into the world. The fourth oval inset from the left in the bottom row frames a young woman looking seriously into the camera. It is labelled, 'Titorenko, R.M.'

It took me weeks of research, thousands of miles of air travel and endless interviews to obtain this picture. Every time I thought I had achieved my objective, something unexpected happened and frustrated my attempt. I *needed* this photograph in order to solve one of the mysteries connected with Russia's First Lady. Every official report, indeed every unofficial report on Raisa Gorbachev's life gives different dates for when she began her course of study at Moscow and when she completed it. This may be a careless omission, or a gap in the facts available which could not be officially admitted for reasons of prestige. Deliberate misinformation cannot be ruled out. What I wanted was irrefutable proof of the actual dates. I didn't want to indulge in any speculation.

In some ways a biographer's task is like that of a doctor. From a number of often vague details provided by the patient, he has to arrive at a diagnosis on which to base the treatment. Probabilities are not adequate to his purpose; he must pursue his researches until he discovers the root cause of the illness. The testimony of a biographer has, similarly, to depend on demonstrable fact. Biographers too must try to lose the word 'probably' from their vocabulary, which is why so much research has to precede actual writing. Things are made much more difficult when the subject of the biography is, for whatever reason, unwilling to talk, and when those around him or her do everything they can to obstruct the biographer in his work.

When I was looking for this photograph, which would provide me with an essential piece of evidence, I discovered that it would vanish immediately from where I could logically expect to find it. This phenomenon seemed almost inexplicable, until somebody in a position to know breached the silence. When her husband was made head of the Kremlin, Raisa Gorbachev demanded the return of all photographs and personal documents relating to her, apart from those belonging to her immediate family. There are, therefore, few people today who can underwrite information about Raisa with authentic photographs. Naturally this leaves the door wide open for the creation of legends, the circulation of half-truths; indeed, complete fabrications are accepted by the public at face value. All of this makes the task of a serious biographer the more difficult. Anyone deterred by the situation ought to leave the job alone.

One fact will not have escaped an observant reader. In the 1954 group photograph Raisa, who had by then been married for a year to Mikhail Gorbachev and was legally 'Raisa Gorbachev', was identified by her maiden name. To find out why her maiden name was used, I put the question to a number of people familiar with Soviet social usages. Briefly, their explanation was that it was normal to use the family names rather than the married names of students in the captions of group photographs at the end of a university course.

Students themselves seldom used family names in ordinary conversation, mainly calling each other by abbreviated versions of their first names and patronymics. Also, in Raisa Maximovna's university days, students frequently married as soon as they could to escape from the extremely puritan, almost cloistered atmosphere of student hostels. As a rule these student marriages did not last long; they were really no more than the formal legalization of the natural sexual drives of young people.

The restrictive legislation of the Stalin era permitted sexual intercourse only between married couples. One consequence of the students' eagerness to get married was an extremely high divorce rate, and quite frequently a rapid second marriage. In order to identify years later the people with whom they had studied, ex-students preferred to have a leaving photograph captioned with the names under which undergraduates had entered university. It was impossible to find out whether those responsible for the 1949–54 group photograph had doubts about the durability of the marriage between Raisa and Mikhail Gorbachev, whether they thought it was just another student affair legalized by marriage. The only indisputable fact remains that when she completed her studies at Moscow State University Raisa Titorenko was actually Mrs Gorbachev.

If a Soviet student wanted to graduate with a good degree in those days, he or she had to demonstrate political commitment. This factor was particularly vital at the time when Raisa Maximovna was attending lectures and seminars in the Faculty of Philosophy at Moscow State University. Even before she was accepted as a university student, the authorities would have positively vetted Raisa Maximovna, calling for her personal dossier and obtaining character references from appropriate people to ensure that she was suitable for a university place.

The gold medal that Raisa received when she left school was only the platform ticket that allowed her to enter the station. It did not permit her to board the university train. For that she needed a specific ticket, and tickets were rationed, like so many things in the USSR, then as now. There were many universities in the Soviet Union, one in almost all the major cities. As a rule, student places were awarded on a basis of political 'pull' ('*blat*') or proximity. Long journeys were to be avoided. Top of the student's list came the university situated in his or her home Soviet republic. A free choice of university was not available to students then any more than it is today. The right to study at Moscow University was proof of real attainment. It showed that

the student was beyond reproach, had demonstrated uncon-
ditional loyalty to the party and the state.

There was, though, one section of society to which the normal
selection procedures for university did not apply: the nomenklatura. Members of this élite had parents, or even grandparents,
whose political and ideological loyalty as 'Old Guard' revolutionaries gave the same status to their descendants. Admission
to the nomenklatura did not depend on the standards by which
ordinary men and women are judged. Medals and distinctions
counted, and relatives in high position in the party bureaucracy.
Raisa Maximovna Titorenko, a railwayman's daughter, had none
of the prerequisites for membership of the nomenklatura, even
though her parents were commendably industrious – their
working day was not limited by an official pay agreement, they
had to fulfil their quota, and this seldom took them less than
twelve hours. The Titorenko parents served the community full-
time, with all their strength. But in contrast to the members of
the nomenklatura, their children were granted no educational
privileges. One of the first articles of the constitution of the new
Soviet society published by Lenin enshrined the right to universal
free education. The state ruled by Stalin did not carry out this
obligation to the letter. In a society founded in theory on principles of equality, some people were more equal than others.

Raisa, whose qualities of leadership had been so apparent even
in childhood to her friend Lydia Budyka, had distinguished herself
at school not just academically but by her outstanding contribution to the activities of the Komsomol, the Communist youth
organization and training-ground for party cadres. Her extreme
shyness was remarked upon, but her social commitment was felt
to be so intense that the authorities responsible judged her worthy
of a university place. Not just at a provincial university, but at
the leading university of the USSR, Moscow State University. It
must be emphasized that Raisa had to compete with rival appli-
cants for university places under a considerable handicap. The
frequent moves of her father in his railway job meant that she
was constantly changing schools, sometimes staying only for a
few months. One consequence was that she was forever having
to offer new proofs of party loyalty. At each new school she
underwent a new assessment, which was filed in her dossier.
Unlike most of her fellow pupils, Raisa could never take a break

from community work. That would have earned her without question a bad report, something difficult to eliminate from her record ...

Moscow, 1949. A lovely evening in late summer. The seventeen-year-old Raisa Titorenko stands with her few belongings at the Byelorussian Station.

A young girl with braided hair, carrying a suitcase much too heavy for her, containing all the possessions she values. A change of clothes for summer and winter, her favourite books, including almost certainly a few textbooks she considers indispensable. Moscow in late summer can be warm, but the nights are cold. Raisa has to take everything.

From the Urals, where she had spent the last year of her school life, to Moscow is a distance of more than 1000 kilometres. For a railwayman's daughter that was not an intimidating journey, nor indeed for a Russian. The vastness of the Soviet Union imposes its own standards of what is near and what is far. Other considerations may have stirred her more: thoughts of home and her parents, and at the same time the overwhelming sensation that she was here at last, here in Moscow, the place she had dreamed about for months, perhaps years.

Raisa had worked hard to see the city where her dreams could come true. She had passed examinations, made sacrifices, undergone investigation and security vetting, made promises, fulfilled every requirement. Admittedly, the gold medal she had won as a school leaver had provided the initial push, but to get the opportunity to study in Moscow she had to reinforce this with favourable references from the Komsomol and other official bodies.

Imagine the scene at the station that summer evening. Thousands of people arrive at the same time as Raisa and press towards the exit. Others are sitting on the platform besides mounds of luggage, waiting for a train whose departure has been announced for that day, but nobody yet knows at what time. The railway staff answer every question with *'budyet, budyet'*, which roughly translated, means: 'patience, patience, it will be here soon.' The young girl from the Altai is not interested in train departures. She stands there, dazed, never having seen such an enormous crowd of people in her life. Suddenly she is swept along, but she

21

manages to cling on to her suitcase and her cardboard box. She keeps reminding herself: 'I must not lose anything.' The most trivial object is irreplaceable. At the front of the station she encounters a similar scene: small armies of people picked up or dropped off by open-topped lorries, while others try to jump on to the running-boards of an already overloaded bus. Rural Russia simply spews people into the capital.

During her long train journey Raisa has read time and again the letter containing her instructions for where to go in Moscow. She knows them by heart, but for the moment she stands, irresolute in the station forecourt. The image she had previously formed of Moscow does not correspond with the reality. Where are the great, brightly-painted houses? The Metro? The happy-looking people, whose faces appear on the front pages of newspapers and the covers of magazines? Where is Red Square, and the Kremlin, where the window of the great and wise Comrade Stalin is lit night and day? All she can see is a landscape of crumbling houses, ruins, bomb craters, painful reminders of the war, disabled men and women. She gradually begins to realize that there is more to Moscow than the view from the station; from where she stands, she can have no conception of the size and scope of the city. She is in a real city for the first time in her life.

Moscow is alien and violent, its streets overflowing with people. Its aggressive individuality and its impressive beauty may well have scared her. Her strongest emotion may equally well have been the excitement of arrival in the big city, the pleasure of anticipation, the longing to be part of Moscow with its Red Square, the Kremlin, its famous departmental store GUM, and the small body of Lenin lying in his mausoleum so near what she had been told were the vast riches of his mind and thought, preserved in the archives of the Lenin Library.

It was to be some months before Raisa began to have any valid insight into what it was actually like to live in Moscow, which for most Russians is the true metropolis of the Soviet Union. The post-war restoration of Moscow was given top priority by the Kremlin. Supplies were more plentiful than in other parts of the country. In downtown Moscow there was food on sale that Raisa had never even heard of: caviare, gammon, prawns, smoked and salted fish ... The prices were, however, so high that students, like most of the city's population, could only press their noses against the shop windows of the delicatessen. It was a familiar student invitation in those days: 'Let's go into the city and feast our eyes.'

The address which Raisa Titorenko had carried to Moscow in her coat pocket and repeated to herself so often on her long train journey, lay in Stromynka Street in Sokolniki, a district in northeast Moscow. It was where the hostel of the Moscow higher educational establishments was to be found. During the reign of Tsar Peter the Great in the seventeenth century, the building had been used as a barracks by the Preobrazhensky Cavalry Regiment. After the 1917 Revolution another storey was built on, probably the last bit of refurbishment that was done to it. The damage suffered by the building in the Second World War was sufficiently limited for the barracks to be used to accommodate post-war students.

Conditions in the hostel were primitive in the extreme. More than ten thousand people lived there, seven to fifteen in a room, with men and women sleeping on different floors of the building. Regulations were strict. Male and female students had to use considerable ingenuity if they wanted to meet. Coded knocks at the door gave warning of visits, and timetables for cleaning the rooms were calculated to give the lovers at least a few minutes together. Not only had the supervisors to be outwitted, but about ten room-mates had to be sent to another room 'on a visit'.

On each floor was a communal lavatory, a wash-basin and rudimentary cooking facilities. Anyone in search of better hygiene had to go to the public baths, and that cost a few roubles and kopecks, which had to be scraped together. The hostel rooms were organized on spartan, military lines, beds for everyone, but tables and chairs did not run to one per student. No cupboards. In every room Lenin looked down from his portrait on the bare wall onto the students below.

Raisa's room accommodated twelve girls. Judged by the standards of the old barracks, it was luxurious. It contained twelve beds, a few bedside tables and one wardrobe, much too small, which held so few of the students' belongings that most personal possessions were kept permanently in suitcases and boxes under the beds. The room had only one table, at which everyone had to sit, presumably not at the same time. Chairs, but never enough

23

for everybody. The walls were panelled in blue, and the windows, left bare, without so much as a net curtain, let in the cold in winter, while in the summer the cramped accommodation made the temperature seem twice as high.

One of Raisa's fellow-students, Ida Ivanovna Schulz, who holds a doctorate in history, gives a first-hand account of life in the hostel: 'I studied with Raisa in the Faculty of Philosophy from 1949 to 1954. I was on the philosophy course, while she read psychology. We lived in one room in the hostel in Stromynka Street, which had been a barracks – in Room 392. Twelve women students lived there together. We were a bit short of space, as you can imagine. The floor was bare concrete, without floorboards or of course a carpet. When we scrubbed the floor, it took three days to dry, we took it in turns to do the cleaning. Although living conditions in our hostel were terribly cramped, we got along together very happily. At the end of the first academic year there were seven of us in one room, then six and eventually four – Raisa, Nina, Khalida Siyatdinova and myself. At midday we ate in the faculty canteen. We weren't too fussy about food; all we wanted was a hot meal. In the evening we made a casserole of potatoes for everybody. Raisa's parents sent us little food parcels. I remember that Raisa and Khalida were sent honey quite often. We shared anything we received between us. We were never actually hungry. Our average grant was about thirty roubles. That was in fact not very much, and many parents helped out with food parcels or a few extra roubles. Dunechka, one of our fellow-students, had no one to support her. So each of us used to put a little money aside regularly to see her through. There were no problems of nationality. We all lived together very content- edly, a girl from Armenia, one from Azerbaijan and one from Uzbekistan.'

There was no system for grouping the students in different rooms; they were quite simply thrown together. They came from all corners of the Soviet Union, and some from satellite countries in the eastern bloc; a few arrived from the West, chosen by their national Communist parties to study in the capital city of the 'true doctrine', the training-ground of party cadres. It was a matter of luck who shared a room with whom; if the management allotted them on any kind of principle, this was never made clear. The only common link was that they were students from the same faculty. The complex financial situation of the students, whose grants barely covered essentials, did lead rapidly to a sense of solidarity. They kept house as a collective, taking it in turns each day to shop and prepare meals. There was seldom any rich food on the table. Usually they had a potato casserole, supplemented with curd cheese and herring. All the students took lunch in the canteen. What was on the menu was less important than the fact that it was a hot meal, generally based on millet or buckwheat. Whoever could guess which was the main ingredient was regarded as a connoisseur.

For the students academic work began at eight o'clock in the morning and continued until five o'clock in the evening, six days a week. They had to leave the hostel in Stromynka Street at seven am at the latest: it was a quick walk to the Metro, by which they travelled to the centre of the city. A few steps from the philosophy faculty building was the university library, in whose large, circular, marble-floored halls the students spent many hours. No student had to be pressed to work hard. To study was an honour and a responsibility. In the library extracts from reference books were copied out, seminar papers written up, examinations prepared for. Overcrowded conditions in the hostel made concentration impossible, so students generally preferred to work in the library. Attendance at all lectures was compulsory; absence without permission incurred disciplinary measures, ranging from a warning about the possible withdrawal of a student's grant to final expulsion.

From Ida Ivanovna Schulz we get a close-up of Raisa's student days: 'From the beginning Raisa received a bigger grant than the rest of us, a reward for the gold medal she won in Krasnodar for her brilliant school results. She did not, however, rest on her laurels; she was extremely single-minded about her studies. We were all young then, just eighteen, but not children. We knew it was our duty to study, and we did that whole-heartedly.

'It really was impossible to work in our room at the hostel, twelve girls in such a tiny space. We only went back there to sleep. We prepared for our seminars in the reading-rooms and university library in Machovaya Street. To make sure of a place you had to get up very early and be outside the library when the reading room opened at 7 am. I often kept a place for Raisa, and sometimes she did the same for me. None of us was lazy, but

25

Raisa was that bit more conscientious than anybody else. We were all children of working-class parents, who had themselves received only a rudimentary education. We wanted to be better educated than they were, to make use of the opportunity we had been given. We arrived from all corners of the USSR, filled with an ambition to conquer the capital.

'We used to prepare for our seminars together. A student well up in a particular subject would test the others in it. Ex-soldiers and officers of the Red Army, who had served at the front in the Great Patriotic War, were members of our study group. They had been demobilized and were equipping themselves for civilian life. They were, of course, older than us and inclined to be patronizing. From our lecture theatre, in which there was, naturally, a large bust of Stalin, we could see the Kremlin. When Stalin died, all the students wept, including Raisa. All of us roommates, including Raisa, stood for two days in the Soyuzov Hall [the Hall of the Trades Unions], where Stalin's body lay on a bier. Raisa caught a really bad cold. During the days of mourning all university work was suspended.'

For the Soviet students at that time life was not all study and political meetings. Nearly all of them had arrived in Moscow from the provinces, and they enjoyed the novelty of participating in city life. Even in Moscow there were shortages of every kind, which people without much money – students among them – had to cope with every day. The capital, more than any other city in the Soviet Union, provided one type of nourishment that made them forget their empty bellies – culture. Although Raisa was one of those students who took her academic work extremely seriously, she still made time to explore this new and unknown city. She quickly discovered that there was far more to Moscow than she had guessed from her first glimpse of an anonymous, overcrowded city when she arrived at the Byelorussian Station. She plunged straight into metropolitan life, getting to know one theatre after another, going to concerts and art exhibitions. Her outlook on life began to widen.

The cultural life of the city undoubtedly cast a glow over the life of Raisa and her fellow-students. We must remember that many of the students were watching an opera or a ballet for the first time. Ulanova, the famous Russian ballerina, was dancing at the Bolshoi then. Her Dying Swan was known throughout the world; it was unique. The students immersed themselves in a whirlpool of discussion about literature and life, argued about authors, lent each other books, sometimes furtively and in secret.

Ida Ivanovna Schulz adds: 'In Moscow we had our first experience of opera, and we saw performances of the highest standard the Soviet Union could then offer. What did we see? The answer is simple. Raisa and I saw pretty well the entire repertoire of the Bolshoi. We heard the most famous singers in the USSR; we saw the most brilliant ballet dancers. We went to the Moscow theatres, too, where we saw the most stunning productions. Through the University Club we took out subscriptions for all Moscow's principal cultural events. The crowds were enormous. Trying to get into an event the normal way, through a box-office booking was almost impossible, the demand was so great. We did manage somehow to get in once or twice a week, to a play, an opera or a concert. Dancing was very popular, especially the tango. I always remember the old tune "Jealousy", one of our favourites.'

Raisa also went to dances organized by the Komsomol. At university balls, the young girl from the Altai with her serious yet serene expression, her thick hair which she wore coiled in a plait on top of her head, attracted many admiring male students. She was a girl who put her whole heart and soul into her dancing. They were all eager to enjoy life, those who belonged to the first post-war generation of Soviet youth. There was a sense of urgency about their activities, as if they were trying to catch up with the time that they and their parents had lost through the war. You did not need to pass a resolution at a meeting of the Komsomol to start a student theatre club. There was a continuous drive towards self-expression, a need for debate about the nature of reality.

Ida Ivanovna Schulz, today a professor of party history at the Technical Institute in Vladimir, east of Moscow, brought to her interview with me one or two old student photographs. 'Oh yes, we had a good time. I can still remember the New Year's Eve party we had in our first year. We took all our beds out of our room and pushed the table into the middle. Raisa Maximovna was wearing a white dress that day. The man in the front wearing boots is Vitya Gorlianski, who is now professor of philosophy at the Conservatory in Gorky. Next to Raisa is Lydia Rusinova, wife of a well-known philosopher, Yuri Levanda. There he is sitting in the front row on the extreme right. Lydia was working in Smolensk until she died in a car crash. Here you can see other friends of Raisa, Ida Solovieva and skinny little Leila Grigorian. In the second row, reading from left to right, Slava Kalinen, who is now on the staff of the news agency, APN; Leonid Chepotarev, he died of cancer; Chamrakol Meltykpotarev from Uzbekistan who is a university lecturer. He was ten years older than the rest of us, and had been chairman of a collective farm for several years before he became a student. That one there, he was a real Count Vronsky. We called him "the Comet". He suddenly appeared on our horizon and disappeared just as quickly. Nina Mordasova and Mirab Mirabmarmadashvili were also part of our group, but they are not in the photograph.

'We all got along together easily, as you can imagine. New Year's Eve was a good excuse for having a meal together, relaxing, having a chat. There were no tensions between us. I remember Raisa that evening in her long white dress, with her slender waist, high heels and hair braided round her head. She was not short of admirers. Although the women philosophy students were all clever and attractive, the men seemed to prefer the psychology students. Why? I don't know. Perhaps psychology students didn't talk so much.

'I remember something else about Raisa. In the first year she wore her hair in long plaits, braided round her head. Then she had it cut off and let it wave naturally. In 1951 she and Nina Mordasova ordered dark blue coats from a tailor's shop not far from the Preobrazhensky hostel. Raisa's coat had a little collar of Persian lamb. Raisa was always very concerned about her friend Nina, who had lived in an orphanage before she came to university. Her only relative, an aunt, worked in the Soviet Embassy in America, and could not give her niece financial support until she returned to the USSR. I myself had to wait a year longer before I could afford a tailor-made coat. Until then I had to make do with a coat belonging to my mother, which I had worn ever since I arrived in Moscow in 1949.

'I recall too that Raisa was very fond of her brother and sister, Genya and Lyudoshka, who were several years younger. Lyudoshka also later studied psychology at Moscow State University, while Genya became a cadet at a military academy.

'In all the years I am talking about, Raisa's parents visited her only once. They slept in the same room as their daughter in the hostel in Stromynka Street, the other students willingly making way for them, as it was to be a short stay. All of Raisa's friends cooked meals for her parents. No one was excluded. All one big family. Most of the students hardly ever saw their own parents, so they were quite pleased and grateful to be able to talk over their problems with surrogate parents. The atmosphere was warm and human; Raisa's father was especially sociable. Raisa's mother sewed on buttons and did some mending for the girls in Raisa's room. Who would have guessed, then, that one day there would be so much interest in Raisa and her life?

'We used to swap clothes regularly. When one girl had a date, the others would offer her their best dresses. A date being something of an occasion, you needed to look your best. Don't forget the boys had quite a lot of choice.

'Raisa was always ready to try something new in her limited spare time. She and Nina Mordasova went on a course of rhythmic gymnastics, which was trendy at the time. Nina had rather a problem with her weight. Unfortunately she got even fatter and had to give the gymnastics up. Raisa carried on with it, as far as I can remember. In her relationships with other girl students Raisa usually took the leading role. She was quick-witted and had fast reactions.

'In 1953 we moved into the new university building in the Lenin Hills. I think we were actually the first students there. We loaded our belongings on to lorries and drove merrily through the whole city. A new university *and* a new hostel, it was like heaven. There were even tablecloths and waiters in the refectory ... While the new university was under construction, all the students from the philosophy faculty were active as party propagandists. We went to the workers – they had all been released from labour camps not long before – and through discussion educated them politically, providing them every week with some background information. Most of the workers, though, were not too keen to talk to us. And when they did tell us something about life in the camps, we quite simply didn't believe them. Quite a few of us thought, in fact, that people who said such bad things about the government belonged in a camp anyway.

'As for Raisa and Mikhail, well, they were very much in love, very happy together. In my opinion they complemented each other ideally. I doubt whether Mikhail Gorbachev would have achieved as much as he has, if he had married somebody else. When Raisa got to know Mikhail she was rather uncertain in her attitude towards men. She had just experienced a somewhat disillusioning love affair. She often asked Nina Mordasova for advice ...

'It was a case of love at first sight for Mikhail Gorbachev, not so for Raisa. He had to court her patiently for a year before she would say yes. Over that year he gave her reassurance, being an intelligent man who inspired confidence. He was strong-willed, impressively serious-minded, an outstanding figure in his student year. He fitted into our circle easily. We liked him. We could see from the beginning what his intentions were regarding Raisa. It's good when a young man behaves like that, isn't it?

'Misha really swam into our ken when we moved to the student hostel on the Lenin Hills. I was already married. My husband brought Misha along. On our floor of the hostel there was round-the-clock security, and nobody, least of all male visitors, was allowed into the rooms. So we met in the common room. I can assure you it was a happy and relaxed wedding party that we, their fellow-students, arranged as our gift to the young couple, Raisa and Misha, in a Moscow University canteen.

'After 1954 I never saw Raisa again, but I do know that Nina Mordasova is still in contact with the Gorbachevs and frequently visited Raisa when they were in Stavropol. She meets Raisa quite often now.

'What else can I tell you about Raisa? I think I've told you everything already. She was open, liked to sing and sang often. She was always humming some tune or other. I remember her as a radiant young woman, full of life, always good-tempered, and who knew how to dress.'

Valentin Sidorov, another of Raisa's fellow-students, a writer whose analyses of Indian philosophy are admired far beyond the frontiers of the Soviet Union, can recall their years together from 1949 to 1954 quite clearly. He was specializing in philosophy, while Raisa was in the other department of the philosophy faculty, that of psychology. Thus they did not meet at lectures, but saw each other daily at the hostel in Stromynka Street. Sidorov remembers vividly what happened when his mother came to visit him unexpectedly during the vacation. There was no hotel accommodation in Moscow, and he was not allowed to let his mother share his room in the hostel. Valentin Sidorov was explaining to his mother that she would have to travel home that same evening, when Raisa intervened and without any fuss gave up her own bed, moving into another room, so that Sidorov's mother had a place to sleep.

Raisa came to Sidorov's rescue more than once. Since she was one of the brightest students in her year and passed all her exams with excellent marks, she received an achievement bonus every month on top of her grant, which was already high on account of her gold medal. So she was financially better off than most of her colleagues. Sidorov borrowed money regularly at the end of the month from Raisa, finding he could not live within his grant. They shared a love of classical music, and they had long discussions about Dostoievsky.

Sidorov also has an unforgettable memory of an evening in June 1954 when their year received their degree diplomas. They wandered all night, happy and relaxed through the streets of Moscow, everyone carrying a candle. For many of her student group it was to be their last meeting with Raisa, who never attended the annual student reunions at the Moskva or the National Hotel. Perhaps it was too long a journey from Stavropol to Moscow, or possibly she had personal reasons for staying away. Who can say for sure?

The most memorable encounter Sidorov had with Raisa was in 1986, when she accompanied her husband, Mikhail Gorbachev, to a writers' congress in Moscow. She recognized her former classmate at once, went over to him and started to talk animatedly about old times. 'We talked just as easily as we used to when we were students,' he said, 'though now I don't have to touch her for the odd rouble.' Although it had been thirty-two years since they last met, Raisa, with her deep interest in literature, had always followed her friend's career as a writer. His books were on her bookshelf, not for show, but because she had read them.

The university life of Raisa Titorenko was not entirely happy and carefree, a time for dancing the tango, going to the theatre and to concerts, taking part in any number of leisure activities. She lived her student days under a sinister shadow, which hung over all of the Soviet Union, including academic life. The slightest

31

breath of dissident thought was pounced on by Stalin and the party and brutally suppressed. Anyone departing from the official orthodoxy was liable to expulsion from university circles, the threat of a slow death in a gulag or immediate execution. The rigid Marxist dogmatism of Stalin had an acutely destructive effect on the study of philosophy. It was forbidden to read the works of Western philosophers, such as Kant and Hegel.

Philosophy was reduced to one crude formula, the struggle between materialism and idealism. Materialism was projected as progressive and forward-looking, idealism was seen as retrograde and reactionary. Marx, Lenin, Engels and Stalin, cult figures in social science, were also regarded as the greatest of philosophers, historians, lawgivers and language experts, and as heroes in other fields.

The development of philosophy in Russia was set back severely. It gave up trying to describe or analyse the world of today. The new task of philosophy was to justify its own existence, in the name of what was officially labelled 'the science of knowledge'. Stalin himself set the ball rolling with his two books, *Marxism and the Study of Language* and *The Economic Problems of Socialism in the USSR*. For years they were taken as models of philosophic thought by whole generations of eastern bloc scholars. This meant that entire areas of social science had to be restructured, causing distortion and deterioration of academic standards.

The imposition of dogma and ideology was not confined to philosophy, but extended to science as well. In biology the teachings of Michurin were supported without reservations. The classical theory of genetics was demolished as a bourgeois half-truth. Its most eminent exponents were denounced as charlatans or smeared as 'bourgeois thinkers'. Stalin himself elevated the suppositions of an uneducated agronomist, Lysenko, about genetic interrelationships, to the status of a science.

Anyone who offered the faintest breath of dissent, who expressed minimal reservations in public, forfeited his university place and his job. Many scientists, who had earlier known international acclaim, found it extremely hard to get work even as street sweepers or unskilled labourers. Some suffered both physical and mental persecution.

This oppressive political and ideological climate must inevitably have affected the young students' attitude to the world and

32

to society. The harsh repression of free thought meant that social behaviour was governed by the need to conform in public, keeping critical opinions hidden. In lectures and seminars every philosophical problem was refracted by the prism of Stalin's work; everything was related to the class struggle and to the party. Academic staff preached a version of Stalinism that was given such a powerful philosophic gloss that students accepted it as the pre-eminent wisdom of their time. Raisa cannot have escaped the influence of all this. Like her colleagues, she expressed her enthusiasm for Stalin's genius, believed implicitly in the imminent victory of Communism, eagerly learned to take quotations from famous Communist writers and use them as a basis for various theoretical constructs. Her diligence and skill in this field earned her a continuous run of good marks and favourable reports.

The spirit of ignorance, dogmatism and scientific amateurism that dominated university life during those years produced, however, a form of hidden protest and ineradicable doubt. Students and staff were aware of the submerged conflict between public and private life, conscious thought and subconscious feelings. There was the additional problem that the calibre of the professors and lecturers was highly variable. The university had on its staff people of outstanding intellectual ability working alongside the most ignorant amateurs. The dean of the Faculty of Philosophy, Professor Molodtsov, for instance, lectured on dialectical materialism and adhered strictly to Stalinist dogma, while the role of guardian of 'intellectual Communism' had been assumed by one Kosichev, who had previously worked as a prison warder in a punishment camp for juvenile delinquents. The lectures on the history of philosophy delivered by M. T. Yofstshuk were based directly on the presumption that Russian philosophy was superior to every other mode of thought.

Among the students with whom Raisa was friendly were Nikolai Ivanovich Lapin, Nail Borisovich Bikkenin and I. Morosova. N. Naumova and Alexander Zinoviev studied with her in the same faculty. Bikkenin and Lapin were both notably hardworking and ostentatiously conformed to party discipline. Although it was repeatedly said later that Raisa had enjoyed friendly personal relationships with everybody in the faculty, it was to Lapin and Bikkenin that she was particularly close. When she had completed her studies, she let many friendships lapse, but she has always maintained regular contact with these two. Their association with the Gorbachev family has done Lapin and Bikkenin no harm.

Lapin, born in 1932, joined the staff of the philosophy faculty magazine, *Voprosy Filosofii* ('Problems of Philosophy'), as scientific editor as soon as he had completed his studies at Moscow State University. He later transferred to the department of sociological research in the Philosophy Institute of the Academy of Science. Soon afterwards he clashed with the director of the Institute, and as a result he was banished for many years to a not very distinguished academic establishment. Lapin's career only began to advance again when Mikhail Gorbachev became General Secretary of the Soviet Communist Party. Although Lapin had scarcely an academic publication to his name, apart from a thin pamphlet – a monograph about the young Marx, in which he had dealt with philosophical questions of no particular significance – he was quite unexpectedly moved from his obscure academic post. He was installed first as Deputy then rapidly promoted to Director of the Philosophy Institute of the Academy of Science. His accelerated promotion had not been anticipated, and it ended as suddenly as it had begun. He was replaced by another man closely associated with the head of the Kremlin, Professor Ivan Timofeyevich Frolov, Gorbachev's adviser on science and culture, who has been editor-in-chief of Soviet Russia's most influential newspaper, *Pravda*, the Party platform, since the autumn of 1989.

Bikkenin, born in 1931, began his career working with Lapin on the editorial staff of the university philosophy magazine, moving from there to the ideology section of the Central Committee of the Communist Party. His principal task was to counter the influence in the USSR of Western thought and attitudes. Since Gorbachev's appointment to the highest office in the Kremlin, Bikkenin has been in charge of *Communist*, the party's ideological weekly. His predecessor in this job was the same Frolov who replaced Lapin. It is difficult to understand what the reformer Mikhail Gorbachev hoped to achieve by entrusting this important position to anyone as cautious and conservative as Bikkenin. Rumours that point to the influence of Raisa in this case have so far not been refuted.

The progress of another of Raisa's contemporaries is equally interesting. Alexander Zinoviev, like Valentin Sidorov, became a writer and an outspoken critic of the social and ideological stances of the Communist Party. His best-known book is his satirical novel *Yawning Heights*, in which he really lays into the Soviet Communist Party for mismanagement and abuse of privilege, attacking not only past leaders but present supporters of *perestroika*. Frolov, for instance, the editor-in-chief of *Pravda*, can plainly be identified. The situation concerning Zinoviev and his book can be regarded as out of character with current Soviet thinking. For while as proof of *glasnost* no subjects are now taboo in Soviet newspapers, Zinoviev's book remains banned and cannot be published, because, I believe, it does not suit Frolov – a real opportunist – or the Soviet comrades within his circle.

Another contemporary, Khalida Siyatdinova, is today professor of philosophy at the party college in Tashkent. She shared a room with Raisa in the university hostel from 1952 to 1954. Khalida lent me a photograph, showing Raisa with the other occupants of the room, and although the picture has faded, you can see that sitting on Raisa's bed is quite a cosmopolitan group. It is remarkable how Raisa always manages to be the centre of attraction, sometimes through a small gesture, the set of her head, or perhaps the dark, spotted dress she is wearing. Whatever the trick is, she has cultivated it and, it would seem, brought it to perfection. In all the many photographs I have studied of Raisa as the wife of the head of the Kremlin, she stands out clearly from the other people in the picture. For instance, the wife of Prime Minister Nikolai Ryzhkov ties a brightly-coloured scarf round her head and wears a coat bought off the peg, but Raisa's clothes are undoubtedly made for her. She has, too, a superior look in her eye. Here are two wives, distinguished from each other not merely by the different status of their husbands, but worlds apart. Raisa is the First Lady in a country which has never defined this as a role, and has never needed to until now.

Raisa's first love was a student named Oleg, a general's son, slim, good-looking, with thick, dark brown hair, who pursued her ardently. They went for long walks together through the parks of Moscow, sometimes just the two of them, sometimes with a girl-friend of Raisa's. It must be remembered that this was a time when conventions were strict in Soviet Russia, which meant that any deep relationship had to lead to marriage. But till then? What should one do till then? The Russians are passionate about walking, which is why lovers are seen wandering through endless, sunlit birch groves in so many Russian films.

The friendship between Raisa and Oleg deepened as they too walked among the birch trees and sat talking on the white, ornate benches of the Moscow parks. Oleg seems to have been the first man who was not deterred by Raisa's feminine reserve to have been allowed to approach her. He eventually made the first move, taking Raisa home to meet his mother. Here he met resistance from the general's wife, who asked where Raisa came from and found that she was the daughter of a railwayman, a quite ordinary railwayman with no social connections, which made Raisa socially unacceptable as the wife of a general's son.

Oleg, a dutiful son, accepted his mother's judgement. He and Raisa never again met on the white park benches.

Raisa and Mikhail Gorbachev met for the first time in 1951, at a student dancing class. Mikhail, who was studying law, had gone along with a friend, to watch him taking part and make fun of him. At their first meeting Raisa took a liking to the good-looking Mikhail, with his boundless self-confidence. But nothing happened. Their friendship did not begin until later. Raisa injured her foot in a gymnastics class and had to be taken to hospital. Mikhail, who had not forgotten their first meeting, visited her there. When the nurses saw him they were impressed and said: 'That's a real heart-throb! Don't let him get away!' And Raisa followed their advice.

Mikhail was not exactly the shy boy from the country with regard to women. It was only when he came to know Raisa that he ended his relationship with his first love Svetlana Koryashkina, who, incidentally, looked very like her. I understand that Raisa can still be quite annoyed if anyone teases her about Svetlana.

Mikhail courted Raisa for about a year, taking her to the theatres, concerts and dances. Together they also took part in student theatricals, which were just starting up on the university scene. He read her poetry in the park and friends say that she awakened his interest in the arts, which he still retains. In the evenings they walked together by candlelight through the streets of Moscow, he carrying the lighted candle that students used to take with them as a symbol of their love. They wanted to get married, but it was now Raisa's parents who advised against it, hoping they would wait until they had completed their studies. But young people have their own way. They insisted on a student wedding, or as the Russians say, a Komsomol wedding. Raisa was twenty-one years old and Mikhail only two years older. They were very much in love. Why shouldn't they get married?

They were married in 1953 in the usual Komsomol style. Neither their parents nor friends from their respective home towns attended the wedding. After the legal marriage ceremony at the city registry office, there was a wedding breakfast for some thirty fellow-students in a corner of the refectory. For once they did not have to drink the usual student tea, which was little more than hot water. Someone had got hold of a samovar and the tea to go with it; there was sausage and salted meat sent by the bride-groom's mother from Privolnoye. Everybody had a good time. Mikhail and his bride left early. Mikhail's room-mates had bil-leted themselves elsewhere, leaving the couple alone for their wedding night, secure in their privacy for those few hours.

The next day things went back to normal. Raisa and Mikhail had to sleep in the rooms on different floors allotted them by the hostel, and this situation continued for about a year. Only then were they permitted as a married couple to share a room together. Mikhail, in their waiting period, sometimes found a way round the problem. Every so often he imposed 'collective sanctions' on his room-mates, which enabled him to spend some time alone with his wife.

In 1954 Mikhail and Raisa Gorbachev moved into the new hostel in the Lenin Hills. Stromynka Street and all its discomforts became a thing of the past. Here they felt they were living in a first-class hotel. The short time that they spent there before leaving Moscow was the happiest time of their student life. Many years later Mikhail said of their time in the Lenin Hills, 'It was unique. I don't think that without that experience my life would have turned out as it has.'

For the Gorbachevs a significant portion of their university life, as for all students, was taken up with what is known in Communist countries as 'community work'. It involved regular attendance at meetings and participation in the campaigns of the Komsomol, taking part in discussions in which the validity of the Communist attitude worldwide had to be affirmed, and, in the years after

Stalin's death, new possibilities for Communism had to be considered. Gorbachev was more active in community work than his wife. He soon became student representative on the faculty management committee of the Komsomol. (I came across an ironic coincidence dating back to this period in his career. Gorbachev was criticized in a newspaper article written by another official named Anatoly Ivanovich Lukyanov, which in itself is nothing unusual, but what is amusing is that today Lukyanov is Gorbachev's number two in the Congress of the People's Deputies.) Raisa undoubtedly carried out all the duties assigned to her within the context of 'community work', but she never actually held office, not even at the most lowly level. That is rather surprising, for at school she was thought to be one of the pupils most active in 'community work'.

In the early years of their marriage, Raisa and Mikhail often went to the cinema. They also attended productions at the Bolshoi Theatre, and at weekends they were often to be found in Luzhniki Park at an open-air concert with a typically mixed Soviet programme of dance, song and orchestral music. Raisa took pains at this time to encourage her husband to take an interest in culture. If at the beginning Mikhail went along mainly to please his wife, gradually he began to appreciate art himself.

Their years at Moscow State University affected the Gorbachevs' lives in several ways. Did they in those early days think about returning eventually to Moscow? Why not? They were both highly qualified Soviet citizens, and in every sense eligible to be summoned back to work in Moscow when things began to open out after the Twentieth Party Congress. Soviet Russia underwent a phase of paralysis, with all political initiative frozen, following the death of Stalin. It took some time for the country to awaken from its deep sleep, and it was during this period of awakening that the Gorbachevs spent their final two years at university. It has to be said here that many Soviet citizens genuinely grieved at the graveside of the dictator, shedding genuine tears. They simply did not want to believe what had secretly been rumoured for years about the machinations of the 'Great Leader'. The poetry of the young Yevgeny Yevtushenko expressed the hopes and desires of the young Russians of this new dawn: hopes of living in a new way, working and loving and travelling in freedom.

It is often artists who, because of their particular sensitivity, act as a kind of seismograph, responsive to latent problems, and therefore appear in the vanguard of progressive movements. Their songs and poems, writings and plays may not actually change anything, but they inspire thought, and sometimes have the effect of a clear mirror, reflecting quite mercilessly society's wrinkles and bald patches.

Raisa finished her course a year ahead of her husband. In her finals she was awarded exceptionally high marks, and the staff of the faculty immediately offered her the chance to continue her academic education through a research fellowship. She would be expected to write a dissertation, a doctoral thesis. Raisa accepted, partly in the hope that it would enable her and her husband to remain in Moscow. This hope was not realized. 'The comrade reflects, the party directs', as the Soviet saying goes, and this was as true for the Gorbachevs as for any other Soviet couple. When he had completed his studies Mikhail was ordered to Stavropol, which meant that Raisa had to postpone for a number of years her ambition of working for a doctorate.

3

Stavropol

In 1955 Mikhail Gorbachev graduated from Moscow State University. But long before he and his wife Raisa received their diplomas, they had to make a decision which would influence the future direction of their careers. Where should they begin their professional lives? New entrants to any profession could not in the Soviet Union in 1955 exercise a choice between various options. All graduates, having enjoyed the special privilege of higher education, had, by a law that still exists, to serve three years in the cadres to which the Soviet government directed them. The principle expressed in the law is simple. The state gives students free education, provides them with accommodation and a grant to live on. The students acknowledge that they have a moral debt to repay to the state. At the beginning of a university course, each student signs a form in which he or she promises to honour the obligation to go wherever the state decrees. Only students who achieve brilliant results or demonstrate what is described as 'exemplary behaviour', meaning of course unquestioning subservience to the party will, can hope to have the slightest influence on their posting. Everything we know about the Gorbachevs indicates that they belonged to this special category. Raisa and Mikhail, as party members who had shown outstanding commitment to the Komsomol, could reasonably have hoped that they would be among those selected to remain in Moscow.

Moscow or a provincial posting? Mikhail was enough of a realist to calculate that there were certain advantages to be gained by being a big fish in a small pond. It was certainly not an easy choice for him or Raisa. Raisa especially was aware that leaving Moscow would be a wrench: no more metropolitan pleasures, no more theatre trips, in exchange for city chic the intellectually stagnant atmosphere of a provincial town. Her years in Moscow had revolutionized what she expected from life; to return to a rural area was for Raisa almost like stepping back into the Middle Ages.

Nevertheless, the Gorbachevs settled for the provinces. Their few possessions were quickly packed, and the train carried the Gorbachevs to a place where they would live for many years, Stavropol, in the south of the USSR. The room they were allocated in Stavropol was little more than a boxroom, small, uncomfortable, without bath or lavatory. When they compared it with the room in which they had just been living at the Moscow hostel, they became vividly conscious of the difference between a capital city and a provincial town. The countryside around Stavropol promised the only consolation. The climate in the Stavropol region on the northern edge of the Caucasus is much milder than that of Moscow. Winter, dreaded in Moscow, lasts only three months. In April southerly winds herald the spring greening of the landscape. The cypress trees which flourish there are a reminder of the Black Sea coast, though it is in fact many kilometres distant. The rural setting is idyllic, with slender trees silhouetted against a purple southern evening sky. Green foliage abounds in Stavropol; in summer it covers the squat houses almost entirely. The attractions of the countryside helped to reconcile the Gorbachevs to their provincial posting, but could not compensate for everything.

Stavropol, whose population was then barely 100,000, was a fusion of town and village. In the town centre were brick houses several storeys high, and metalled roads. But away from the centre the atmosphere became ever more countrified, populated by houses with small, enclosed gardens, where the occupants grew their own vegetables. Most of the families were of peasant stock and retained some peasant traits. If they happened to have a surplus of a garden crop, they sold it in the market, which had evolved over the years into a social centre for these unsophisticated people. They went to market not just to buy and sell, but to hear news, to exchange information about everyday things – in short, to have a good gossip.

The region in which Raisa and Mikhail now lived, partly from choice, partly through an official directive, was not greatly different from many others in the vast Soviet Union, except in one unusual geographical feature, which was to have its influence on the Gorbachevs' future career. Stavropol is at the heart of a cluster of natural springs, whose waters are said to have the power to heal a range of physical ailments. Places like Mineralniye Vody, Pyatigorsk and Kislovodsk, which all lie within the Stavropol region, had a high reputation as health resorts in the time of the tsars and have retained this under the Soviet regime. The construction of new sanatoria is constantly in train. Many Soviet leaders have come to Stavropol to take the waters. Some eighty sanatoria and more than twenty residential hospices offer cures for alcoholism, mudpack treatment or hydrotherapy. Special élite health establishments for the government and the party, which the ordinary Soviet citizen cannot enter, are concentrated in the Stavropol region. As in the days of the tsarist aristocracy before the Revolution, Kremlin leaders, ministers, influential party bosses, editors of important newspapers, field marshals and generals with their wives and children all come to take the waters. In Kislovodsk there are, for example, special sanatoria exclusive to the higher ranks of the Soviet armed forces and dachas for the KGB.

The Stavropol mineral waters proved doubly valuable to the Gorbachevs, not only helping to keep them fit, but also assisting their climb up the Soviet career ladder. One of the duties of the party chief of the Stavropol region was to look after important guests from Moscow. These VIP's often spent the whole of their leave in the region and would frequently send for the local party leader to keep them company. Mikhail Gorbachev, as the party boss in Stavropol, thus became more familiar with influential party leaders than any party official of equivalent rank. The Gorbachevs, as might be expected, took their duties of hospitality very seriously. It was protocol for Raisa, as the wife of the local First Secretary, to accompany her husband on these occasions. Both Mikhail and his wife soon began to make a favourable impression on their Kremlin guests, and to have increasing contact with them.

One of the VIPs was Yuri Andropov, the KGB chief under Brezhnev. Andropov, normally an aloof personality, recognized early on that the Stavropol regional secretary had unusual qualities marking him out for promotion. In the ensuing years Andropov became an advocate for both Raisa and Mikhail Gorbachev. It was not just Mikhail's intellectual ability that attracted Andropov's attention; he was, it is generally thought, impressed by Raisa's capacities. She represented a new type of woman for the old Communist from Moscow, sufficiently educated to step out of the shadow of her husband and play a social role of her own. She was the kind of wife who, in the best sense of that word, *supported* her husband; she did not hold him back or become a burden to him. It is possible that Raisa revived for Andropov memories of Krupskaya, the woman without whom Lenin, the father of the Soviet state, might never have achieved his life's work. In a way tradition and progress came full circle, something that was to recur quite often in the life of Raisa Gorbachev. These are circumstances, however, that belong to the future. At this point the Gorbachevs still occupy only the first rung on the promotion ladder of Soviet bureaucracy. They are beginning to settle down in Stavropol.

Mikhail Gorbachev was deputy head of the agitprop department of the Komsomol in the town, and Raisa obtained a post as tutor in philosophy at the Stavropol Agricultural Institute. She did not apply for this appointment, having been assigned to the post by Moscow. It should be pointed out that although she had studied philosophy at university, her main subject had been psychology. She began at the Institute in Stavropol by leading seminars, on the lowest rung of the academic ladder.

Over thirty years later, her friend Lydia Budyka says: 'She has always worked hard, having a conscientious temperament. As a result of her preparations for the seminars and her subsequent position as a lecturer she accumulated mountains of books at home for study. As long as I can remember she has talked incessantly about her work, what she has to do, how she must prepare for a lecture, which book she must read, how busy she is . . . ' The ability to run her home, spend many hours in discussion with Mikhail Gorbachev, prepare for seminars and work at the Institute must have called for plenty of self-discipline from Raisa.

Raisa went to the market almost every day, not so much to

hear the local gossip as to buy food for her household. The Gorbachevs did not have a garden, which would have provided them with soft fruit and vegetables, and prices in the shops were much higher than those in the market. The rich soil of southern Russia produced a modest surplus in comparison with many other regions of the Soviet Union. Sheep farmers from the foothills of the Caucasus supplied the market with meat, milk and cheese, while farming families from the old Cossack villages specialized in rearing beef and dairy cattle. For the first time in their married life, the Gorbachevs had sufficient meat for a good table. The food situation was, in fact, so much better than in Moscow, that it must to some extent have compensated Raisa as a young housewife for the city amenities she had lost. The price of fruit and vegetables in Stavropol enabled Raisa to indulge her ideas of a healthy diet. Fruit and vegetables were served in various forms almost every day in the Gorbachevs' house. In contrast to traditional Russian housewives, Raisa cut out foods rich in fats or carbohydrates, and she still does so today.

Their daily life became noticeably more comfortable, when Mikhail was promoted to the nomenklatura. He had, as First Secretary of the Stavropol Komsomol Committee, a staff car at his disposal, which his wife could also use for her shopping in the market. Despite the improvement in her material situation, however, Raisa continued to compare life in the sleepy, provincial backwater of Stavropol with the social richness of Moscow. Although as students the Gorbachevs had been permanently handicapped by lack of funds, they had both benefited significantly from the cultural opportunities available to them in Moscow.

Mikhail adjusted more easily than Raisa to Stavropol's living conditions, which may partly be due to the fact that he was in a sense at home. He had, after all, spent his childhood and youth in the region. He had certainly enjoyed university life in Moscow, but it had been for him simply a phase in his career. Nor did the cultural stagnation of Stavropol worry him. He had his work, which he found absorbing, and nothing much else impinged on him. His attitude could on occasion provoke fierce emotional reactions from his wife, in their first years in the provinces. She simply would not accept his phlegmatic approach to life in Stavropol. She influenced Mikhail in two ways. She fired him with her conviction that he must never rest satisfied with his professional achievements, and at the same time she impressed on him that while work is important, it is not all-important. Any account of the career development of Mikhail Gorbachev must acknowledge the importance of Raisa's influence. She has to be given credit for encouraging her husband to develop his talents to the full. It is of course pointless to imagine how his life might have worked out without the resolute Raisa in the background. It must be stressed emphatically that the support she gave him cannot be exaggerated, though his professional achievement remained his own.

When Mikhail became First Secretary of the Stavropol Komsomol Committee, he became entitled not just to a staff car, but also to a well-furnished apartment. Doors to shops and businesses reserved for the nomenklatura were now open to the Gorbachevs. Their holiday problem was solved. In their first years in Stavropol, they had not been permitted to leave the town, something which Raisa at least regarded as a form of exile, but now Mikhail's official position gave them access to the most desirable spas and resorts in the USSR.

Official leave, and the occasional trip to Moscow on which Raisa could accompany her husband, were the only breaks in a year dominated by the demands of work. Mikhail disappeared into his office from early morning until late at night, or paid a visit to one of the youth organizations which were part of his portfolio of party responsibility. Raisa was left to manage the details of their domestic life.

The loneliness of Raisa's first years in Stavropol have remained a memory she dislikes recalling even now.

An important milestone in the lives of the Gorbachevs was the birth of their daughter Irina Mikhailovna on 6 January 1957.

The great Russian democrat and philosopher Alexander Herzen says that a woman who has borne a child becomes automatically a state employee, for becoming a mother is a woman's primary social function. This idealistic theory contrasts starkly with Soviet reality. For millions of women in the Soviet Union at that time, the joys of motherhood were overshadowed by the hardships of coping with everyday life, indeed of ensuring survival. Few mothers could manage to interrupt their paid work for long, once their child was born. It was not only a question of money, which a woman lost by taking maternity leave. What mattered far more was the fact that the issue of ration books and food coupons was linked to employment. Anyone who did not work had to survive without these necessary documents and make do with income support, which was often inadequate. Not many mothers felt after the birth of a child that they were 'government employees' in the sense Alexander Herzen meant.

Raisa was able to look after her daughter herself without these problems, thanks to her husband's high-ranking position in the Stavropol bureaucracy, and also to his membership of the nomen-klatura, which was, admittedly, at this stage of his career at a fairly humble level. The privileges that Raisa took for granted in Stavropol did not extend beyond the region. Friends can recall that the wife of the Stavropol Komsomol Secretary was treated in Moscow children's wear stores like any other housewife. She had to queue up for rompers and outdoor clothes and must often have known the experience of waiting in a queue for a long time, only to come away empty-handed.

Raisa is apparently one of those reasonable mothers, who don't shout or become hysterical, but keep themselves and their child under control calmly but firmly. Her friends still smile about the incident with Irina at a reception for International Women's Day on 8 March many years ago, to which children were invited. There were good things to eat on the table and before the official speeches were even under way little Irina began to tuck into the food, ignoring everyone else. Her mother called her name in a sharp, clear voice of command that carried across the hall. Irina immediately dropped everything and hid herself behind the curtains. Her mother, without raising her voice or moving a step, had called the child to order.

Her share in these experiences should not delude us into thinking of Raisa as the archetypal Russian woman. She is the First Lady of a country, which even today does not allow other women the chance to use her as a role model. Her image and reality are out of reach for ordinary Russian women and likely to remain so in the foreseeable future. The extensive popularity that her husband enjoys in the Soviet Union does not automatically include his wife. Women workers in factories or collective farms, who meet Raisa on her travels through the USSR, tend to look at her with envious eyes. They feel she is too remote, that she

47

ought to be setting an example as a wife and mother. They know that, even in the biggest stores in Moscow, the clothes and accessories Raisa wears with such flair are not available to the general public. There is an authenticated story about the Gorbachevs' visit to a certain town, where women with only two dresses in their entire wardrobe commented sardonically on the fact that Raisa changed her outfit twice during the visit.

After the birth of her daughter, Raisa's life in the provinces gradually changed. She became more extrovert and sociable, accepting invitations more readily for trips to the Caucasus Mountains or the shores of the Black Sea. It was, however, always with the same group of people. Life in the nomenklatura had its own unwritten rules, dictating which contacts were acceptable, which not.

Lydia Alexandrovna Budyka has been a friend of Raisa's for many years, and gave me some of my most productive interviews. She was, however, only willing to talk within certain constraints. Following each interview she had to refer back to Raisa, who was not always available, or Lydia Budyka failed to contact her, or the message came that Raisa did not want this or that fact to be made public, or this or that photograph to be published. Lydia Budyka is a pediatrician, who treated Raisa's daughter regularly when she was ill. In the Stavropol years, when they were close friends with the Gorbachevs, her husband was Secretary of Agriculture on the City Committee, making him a colleague of Mikhail Gorbachev. Their friendship has endured, though naturally they see each other less often now that Mikhail Gorbachev has become President. Lydia finds she has to phone several times before she is put through to the First Lady.

Lydia looks back on the Stavropol years with pleasure: 'Life was freer, as it often is in the provinces, more open. Mikhail had his work for the Komsomol and also his party work, and there was a large circle of friends. We were all young and sociable and enjoyed being young together. We celebrated all the main Soviet public holidays together, usually in a sizeable group. We all used to meet at each other's houses and listen to music. We were all working, men and women, and we would go round after work to somebody's place where all the women would make *pilmeni*,* sometimes the men too. It was an honest, open and happy life.'

* a kind of meat dumpling or ravioli

The Gorbachevs and the Budykas got to know each other on excursions to Lake Seyengileyevskoye, a beauty spot some ten kilometres outside Stavropol. 'On Sundays our husbands would drive out there with us to relax. They worked together during the week, so we went out together at weekends, taking the children, and generally getting to know each other. We had a wonderful time.

'The Gorbachevs are an exceptionally honourable couple, intelligent and true to their principles, and being in their company gave me a great deal. Mikhail Gorbachev is an amazing person; Raisa, too. They lived in Stavropol just like ordinary people, quite simply. They were sociable and had a large circle of friends. Their situation has changed, inevitably, and his enormous work-load obviously imposes a more restricted lifestyle on them. Raisa herself has always been a good friend to me, and what impresses me most today is that so far as I'm concerned she hasn't changed in the slightest. I can still give her my opinion on a whole range of things, knowing she will listen to me, although whether we agree or not is another question. We have a really good relation-ship, a genuine friendship.'

The Gorbachevs' love of the countryside, their liking, which they still retain, for long country walks, was something they could indulge in Stavropol. On Sundays senior officials used to drive off in their staff cars into the country, where they would meet colleagues and their families at a prearranged rendezvous, at which food and drink would be ready in large picnic hampers. The group would walk for twenty or thirty kilometres, there would be a singsong, photographs would be taken of them eating, drinking and having family fun. Raisa's friends still recall her powers of endurance, especially when climbing in the mountains. While most women, breathless because they were overweight, pleaded for the climb to end, Raisa would not give up until they had reached the summit.

In photographs taken of her at that time she is the epitome of a type of Russian woman you can see throughout the Soviet Union, sturdy, with short, powerful limbs. Her reddish-brown hair looks rather longer than today, though it has evidently been styled by a hairdresser. She is not so different from her rather overweight women friends, her face is plump, and I would guess she weighed some twenty pounds more than she does now.

Certainly she was a long way from the sophisticated look she acquired from her European travels.

Most of the other nomenklatura wives, with whom Raisa spent her afternoons and weekends, were far inferior to her intellectually. She had to endure boring conversations about trivialities. If the topic of the latest local drama production came up, it was in terms of which dress this wife or that wife had worn to the theatre. Only one or two wives could express an intelligent opinion on the plays, which were almost invariably mediocre, or the cast. Raisa had little contact with the intelligentsia of the region – the group drawn from the teaching staff of agricultural, educational and medical institutions located in Stavropol – since the code of the nomenklatura allowed free association with members of these establishments only in exceptional cases. Progressive ideas, especially in the arts, had not reached Stavropol, or, for that matter, many provincial regions of the USSR. The atmosphere was conservative and stuffy. Things which had been everyday currency in Moscow, Leningrad, Kiev and the other great cities of the Soviet Union for years had simply not arrived in Stavropol.

The usual range of newspapers and periodicals was available, and books too; those the Gorbachevs could not get, friends sent them from Moscow. Khrushchev's exposure of Stalin's regime at the Twentieth Party Congress had brought a new spring to the Russian literary world. Books which for many years had had to be kept hidden suddenly appeared, and an increasing number of writers had the courage to introduce new ways of looking at history. The poems of Anna Akhmatova were published and the diaries of Blok printed; Solzhenitsyn and Granin examined the gulag system. After years of physical and psychological terror the effect was sensational. It was a liberation that unleashed immense spiritual energy.

Raisa read many books on many subjects, but she did not find anyone within the nomenklatura in Stavropol with whom she could discuss them. The intellectual gulf was too great for any serious talk about literature to be possible. But in Mikhail she had at least a patient listener. A pattern was established which the Gorbachevs still follow. Raisa would give her husband a detailed summary of her reading, and suggest to him which books he ought to read for himself. The Gorbachevs found a means of intelligent, intimate communication, which was not available within the narrow confines of the local nomenklatura.

The higher Mikhail moved up the ladder of power, and the longer the marriage lasted, the more time they had to spend apart. The energy of this undoubtedly remarkable women, her drive to stay at the centre of the action, to keep in touch with clever and intelligent people, is underlined by the fact that during those Stavropol years she laid a practical foundation for exploiting effectively her active, creative talents. After the demanding, lively years at Moscow University she found herself not only a resident of a small provincial town, but enclosed in a particularly conservative segment of its society. The personal cost to Raisa of admission to the closed ranks of the nomenklatura is hard to estimate. What is certain is that Raisa integrated herself into this world and learned to live with its unwritten rules, which are almost as complicated and numerous for a party official's wife as for the official himself.

What were these regulations, these unwritten laws governing the nomenklatura?

The first concerned the hierarchical subordination, or 'pecking order' of younger people in relation to older members. The Secretary of the City Komsomol Committee did not consider himself as equal in rank to the Secretary of the City Party Committee, which meant that his wife had a social status inferior to that of the senior official's wife. Within the nomenklatura wives accepted that they occupied the place in the hierarchy defined by their husband's professional function. Hierarchical distinctions were sacrosanct and not to be ignored under any circumstances. Any attempt to evade the distinctions in the slightest brought serious consequences. A wife could find herself ostracized by other wives, inevitably damaging her husband's career prospects.

The second revolved round compulsory association. Like the husbands, whose personal contacts depended exclusively on the requirements of their jobs and careers, with the result that social relationships seldom extended beyond the tight circle of the nomenklatura, the wives were expected to live within the same social limits. Personal feelings and friendships were irrelevant. The only consideration for a wife was her husband's personal ambition. An invitation to tea from the wife of a superior was regarded as a command, even when the junior wife knew that this would involve her in an extremely boring afternoon. The system also worked in reverse. You could not say: 'Let's go to the Petrovs. They always have something interesting to talk about,' if the Petrovs were not among the acceptable social contacts. Invitations were routinely given or accepted; you had to attend or offer hospitality. Personal choice was only a minimal factor in social activities. Participation was what mattered.

The third rule governing social life in Stavropol decreed: 'In no circumstances give yourself airs.' The rule defined the wifely stance precisely, indicating the conduct expected of a wife at the receptions and public occasions when protocol allowed her to accompany her husband. At these party receptions the table was invariably groaning under the weight of food and drink and the speeches went on and on all evening. Every speaker, almost without exception, proposed a wordy toast, to which the guests responded by downing 100 grammes of vodka. Women were not exempt from the vodka ritual and they had to exercise some wit and ingenuity to emerge from the evening sober. Nor was it just the vodka that made these occasions a strain for an intelligent woman. A wife was barred by patriarchal tradition from taking part in the male discussion, and it would have been regarded as unseemly for her to advance any view related to her husband's work, or express any opinion on decisions of the regional party leadership, or any comment on top-level politics. At party social events the husband was left to give a solo performance. Married couples could not play a harmonious duet; the interplay between husband and wife as equal partners was not possible under the rigid nomenklatura code.

All this placed particularly heavy demands on an intelligent woman like Raisa, imposing a denial of her entire being and creating urgent problems of self-discipline. She constantly had to repress an impulse to cut in on the maundering reflections of men who had had too much to drink. She would have liked to describe to mentally torpid nomenklatura of Stavropol the actual living conditions of the people of the region, backing up her views with accurate statistics. In fact the population knew the 'Promised Land' of Communism only from what they had heard of Lenin's dreams and the agitprop of his disciples; their life went on much as it had done under the tsars. Raisa had, however, to live within the inflexible rules of the nomenklatura, fully aware that one breach of them could have meant the end of Mikhail's career.

Raisa used the limited time she had when her husband was home to inform him of what she had discovered while researching her doctoral thesis in sociology on the actual situation in the local rural area, the reality obscured by party promises. She explained what she saw as essential preliminary measures to improve things. Her intense preoccupation with both theoretical and practical questions of sociology, which we shall discuss more fully later, were early on put at Mikhail's service. Their home became a forum, a valuable source of ideas for his political decisions. Raisa was, unofficially, a principal adviser to her husband on the social conditions of the people for whom he was administratively responsible. Only because there was no alternative did she submit to the unwritten rules of the Stavropol nomenklatura, and even these did not curb her spirit. She retained, in spite of everything, her sense of what was feasible and vital under existing political conditions. She kept her imagination alive, as I have stressed, through a constant exchange of ideas with her husband at home.

Let us return once more to the communal life of the nomenklatura in Stavropol in the Fifties, which was not solely a matter of rules and prohibitions. There were some positive features, such as the prevalent hospitality. The families of the closed nomenklatura circle frequently exchanged visits among themselves, and had established a tradition of lavish hospitality. You were not invited for a cup of tea and a bun, you were entertained first to lunch and then to an elaborate evening meal with several courses of rich dishes, and you were, of course, well wined. Stavropol produced good wine from its own vineyards, but the really special wines served came from neighbouring Georgia.

A hostess seldom had problems obtaining supplies on a grander than usual scale for a nomenklatura party. Most of the top people with jobs in the city of Stravropol itself had 'arrangements' with the chairman of a collective farm or the secretary of a rural district committee of the Komsomol or of the party. Efficient personal supply lines ran between the city and the rural administrations, working on the principle of 'You scratch my back, and I'll scratch yours.' Under another unwritten rule, members of the leadership in the city were provided every month with not only a regular delivery of meat, poultry, fruit and vegetables, but also seasonal delicacies. In the autumn they got freshly caught fish from the clear streams of the region, and in the winter, after the pigs had been slaughtered, the rural officials had carefully prepared gourmet garlic sausages delivered to their comrades in the city. Only the tenderest meat was good enough for these sausages.

Scarcity was unknown to the families of the nomenklatura, even when poor harvests brought serious food shortages to the homes of local people. The larders of senior officials remained well stocked; the differences between officialdom and the ordinary citizen were at their most marked in the realm of food. Even keeping food fresh presented few problems to an official's family. They had no freezers or refrigerators then, but their houses were built with deep, cool cellars, where food could safely be stored for long periods.

The Gorbachevs' table, too, was richly spread, especially when they were doing some official entertaining. They could always celebrate Russian festivals with appropriate meals – 1 May, Revolution Day (7 November), New Year's Day or the birthdays of members of the family. Food supplies from country to town suffered a continuing decline for many years, but a nomenklatura family was scarcely aware of the problem. They lived in a Communist paradise with many amenities.

A superior supply of food was not the only privilege enjoyed by the nomenklatura. At that time the fashion-consciousness of Soviet women was dictated not so much by their tastes in dress as by what was available. Nomenklatura wives had, in general, a far better chance than ordinary housewives of obtaining lengths of scarce material from shops. It was one of their duties to project an attractive personal image, and they duly received a subsidy to achieve this. In matters of fashion and dress the strict hierarchy of rank had to be maintained, and here again everything depended on the husband's professional status. It meant, quite literally, that the wife of a junior official must never be better dressed than the wife of his superior. The hierarchical lines were as rigidly drawn in fashion as anywhere else, with dire consequences for any nomenklatura wife breaking ranks. Clothes that were individual, or related to European fashion in any way, could seldom be acquired. The hallmark of Soviet clothes for many years was that they were decidedly boring.

If women's fashions were merely boring, men's clothes were like a party uniform. Autumn, winter and spring Mikhail and his fellow administrators wore navy blue, black or charcoal grey gabardine suits. Their long, heavy winter coats were also made of sombrely-coloured material, and fastened at the neck with a short fur collar. The winter fur hat, which was also obligatory, was exchanged in the warmer months in favour of a shapeless felt hat. In summer the nomenklatura 'uniform' consisted of a light grey suit, worn with a white shirt and tie. A straw hat protected them in the height of summer from sunburn or heat stroke.

Photographs show that in winter in Stavropol Raisa usually wore a quilted coat with a fur collar and fur trimming on the sleeves. She set her fur hat at a provocative angle. She also wore suede or fur-lined leather ankle-boots. Women did not wear knee-length boots until well into the 1960s; more precisely, these were not produced as fashion goods until then.

Raisa's everyday wear was usually a severely cut suit and a white blouse, which was always fastened with an expensive brooch. Her evening clothes were dark, unobtrusive, often made of brocade or velvet. In summer Stavropol's warm climate dictated the choice of clothes. The material used for lightweight suits or day dresses was bright and vivid, in keeping with the cheerful colours of the countryside.

Designer clothes, a rarity at that time, were not available to the women of the nomenklatura. Everything they wore was made individually for them. Even when it came to choosing shoes, these women did not have to depend on what was in the shops. In every region of the Soviet Union there were small workshops, whose entire production was exclusively for the ruling class. It was, of course, the same in Stavropol. The tastes of the élite clientele were well-known in these workshops, where the aim was to give special satisfaction to those wives whose husbands held senior rank.

Living in a relatively isolated part of the country made it difficult for women to compare notes; they had to arrive at a particular style themselves. There were no fashion magazines to consult. People wore what they liked, whether it was fashionable or not. Naturally they wanted a style that distinguished them in some way from the wives of other officials. However, the unbalanced diet, over-rich in fat and carbohydrates, served in the homes of most officials, the sameness of lifestyle and the substantial fare at parties combined to produce women inclined to plumpness at a quite early age. This naturally restricted their choice of clothes. Although Raisa took great pains to arrange a healthy diet for her family, photographs from the early years of her marriage provide evidence that the opulent banquets left their mark on her as well. She managed to avoid the worst, but her figure did have something of the ample lines of other officials' wives.

It was not until the Twentieth Party Congress in 1956 that changes in social habits, in keeping with the relative liberalization of the political scene, began to occur. Contact with the outside world increased. Closer relationships with neighbouring Soviet republics became possible, and in exceptional circumstances visits to Moscow. Gradually the Moscow leadership entrusted some assignments involving travel abroad to regional party officials. Standards were no longer laid down on a regional basis, and 'comparability' became a buzz-word. The Stavropol ruling class began to recognize that living standards in some Soviet satellite countries were quite often higher than in Russia. They also noticed that ordinary housewives were better dressed than in the Soviet Union.

Another factor emerged to relieve the ennui of provincial life. Soviet troops had been stationed in the countries of the eastern bloc since the end of World War Two, to underpin the Communist governments. Officers had been allowed to have their families with them, and their wives began to return to Russia with some surprising information. In spite of shortages prevalent in the satellite countries in the post-war years, there were consumer goods on sale there which had not even been heard of in the Soviet Union. The army wives who had been stationed in East Germany regularly brought home in their travel chests and suit-cases 'treasures' which sparked envy among home-based officials' wives, who had remained largely insulated from the outside world. Their experience hardly reached beyond the frontiers of their region, and the circles in which they moved were still narrow, in spite of the greater general openness in Russia. Nomen-klatura wives spent their leave with their opposite numbers in the same sanatoria and health resorts. Their families had medical treatment in the same clinics, built specifically for them. Their apartments all had furnishings made in the same Soviet factory. The children went to specially privileged schools, being driven to

The world of little Raya Titorenko. Raisa spent the first two years of her life in a railway settlement in the small town of Vessolayarsk in the Altai Mountains. She has no memory of Vessolayarsk. This picture recalls her childhood lived in a goods wagon in obscure places like Vessolayarsk.

Raisa Titorenko, a teenager with an expression out of an old Hollywood film. She seems to be in a dream – perhaps of becoming the wife of the President of the USSR?

Above A class photo of the Philosophy Faculty of Moscow State University, of those who graduated in 1954. All the tutors and Raisa's fellow-students are in the picture.

Right Detail: fourth from left in bottom row is Raisa Titorenko. In fact, long before the end of the course, Raisa had ceased to be called Titorenko and had taken the name of Gorbachev.

Raisa's room and her roommates in 1949. Raisa in the middle, on the right is Nina Lyakicheva, and on the left Ida Schulz.

Above 'Nothing gets us roommates down.' From left to right: Ida Schulz, Raisa, Siran Arut, Nina Lyakicheva. Khalida Siyatdinova.

1951: Raisa and Nina Lyakicheva – two friends outside the children's home where Nina was brought up.

Right Oleg is not a bad photographer. Raisa and her friend Khalida Siyatdinova pose for him happily. Oleg has picked flowers for Raisa, who gazes demurely down.

Left Spring 1950: First love in Moscow, where Raisa and Oleg lingered for hours on park benches. Raisa and Khalida were happy to be photographed beside the good-looking Oleg, but who would have guessed at this time that Oleg would one day be proud to have been friendly with the wife of the President of the USSR?

Left Mikhail Gorbachev with his girlfriend Svetlana taking part in an amateur dramatic production in Stavropol in 1949. When Mikhail met Raisa, he said goodbye to Svetlana.

Right Oleg and Svetlana belong to the past. Sociology student Raisa and law student Mikhail marry on 25 September 1953.

Above Stavropol, 1967: staff of the Faculty of Marxist-Leninist Philosophy pass their exams. Left to right: A. M. Charlamov; S. P. Shaparalov, head of the examining board; J. M. Alshanki; Raisa; N. Shaskov, today professor at the State University of Kishinev; F. Yarovaya, a laboratory technician.

Left G. V. Osipov, Raisa's supervisor for her doctorate, proudly shows me where he used to meet his pupil, when sociology was 'relegated to the cellar' at 16 Pizova Street, Moscow. It is not marked today.

Professor Vladimir Spiridonovich Gott at the reading of Raisa Gorbachev's dissertation. Gott directed the preparation of this dissertation from 1965–67.

Above Congress of the school brigades in Stavropol, 1963. Raisa is second from left. Third from right is the cosmonaut V. Bykovski.

Raisa with members of the academic staff of the Stavropol Agricultural Institute, where she was a lecturer. Behind her is G. S. Dimitriyev.

Football at a picnic near Stavropol in the Sixties. Raisa demonstrates her skill at rhythmic gymnastics. Next to her is Popov, the Chairman of the Regional Party Committee in Stavropol.

'It ought to be grilled.' Mikhail and Alexander Budyka, head of the Economic Section of the Party Committee, Stavropol region, grill kebabs over the fire. Third from left is Lydia Budyka, sixth from left is Raisa.

Young Pioneers' Camp near Stavropol, with a campfire atmosphere.
Galina Vassilenko, teacher and wife of the Second Secretary of the regional
Komsomol committee; Lydia Budyka with her husband, Alexander;
Tamara Rybina, a doctor; Raisa and Mikhail Gorbachev.

Another pose for the family album? Raisa, whose new slogan was 'As far
as my legs will carry me', with Tamara and Lydia.

Right If you think from the clothes that this is a typical teenager from the West, you are wrong. This is Irina Gorbachev in April 1974, on her first trip abroad. She was accompanying her father on his first trip to East Germany.

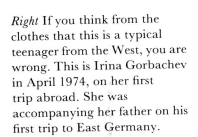

Left Irina, only daughter of the First Family of Stavropol, is married in May 1977 to Anatoly Verganski. The wedding is Stavropol's social event of the year.

1983: New Year's Day for the Party Secretaries. A New Year's morning stroll through snow-covered Pyatigorsk. From right: Mikhail; Irina; Boldyrev, First Secretary of the City Committee of Pyatigorsk; Anatoly; Inshiyevski, First Secretary of the Regional Committee of Karachevo; Raisa and Madame Inshiyevski; Alla Ivanovna Kasnacheyeva and her husband Viktor, Second Secretary of the Regional Committee of Stavropol; and Alexander Raspopov, First Secretary of the Town Committee of Kislovodsk, with his wife.

Above 'On with the walk, Party Secretaries!' In the background is the government dacha in the Caucasus mountains, scene of the New Year's Day celebrations.

Anatoly took this picture of his wife Irina on the New Year's Day walk.

Above Pyatigorsk, 1973: Raisa's apprenticeship in diplomatic duties. As wife of the First Secretary of the Regional Committee of the Communist Party in Stavropol, she gives an official send-off to the wife of the Bulgarian ambassador to the USSR, D. Zhulev.

Right Moscow, Alexei Tolstoy Street. The Gorbachevs lived on the seventh floor from 1968 to 1971. Today the apartment looks empty and forbidding.

Below Raisa at a reception in the Palace of Congresses at the Kremlin, before her husband became General Secretary. On the left is Madame Ryzhkov, wife of the present Prime Minister Nikolai Ryshkov.

and from school in their father's official car. The younger generation in politics was invariably recruited from the same social group, representing a form of professional inbreeding which could only seldom be breached by outsiders.

The living arrangements of the Gorbachevs in the period under review cannot legitimately be compared with what would have generally been considered acceptable in the West. Their home ran efficiently and was expressive of their social status, but certain features in it bore the Gorbachev hallmark. The Gorbachevs had quite early in their married life acquired a piano, at which their daughter Irina was later to spend many hours. Another noticeable feature was the number of books. The living-room and bedroom of their apartment looked like a library, largely because of Raisa Gorbachev's interests. Raisa carefully supervised the lending and return of books and took pains to add to their collection. She could always have borrowed books from a lending library, but friends from her Stavropol days say that Raisa was more often to be found in a bookshop than a library. Books were an essential in her life, as indeed they are today. She does not confine herself to books that are professionally useful to her; she enjoys literature and the arts. Raisa seldom lets an evening pass without some reading.

The Gorbachevs used to relax in one of a group of dachas, set in delightful woodland scenery, with a friendly stream meandering through it, not far from Stavropol itself. All the party officials had their dachas there, each furnished to the standard of comfort appropriate to their rank in the nomenklatura. Differences in status were still strictly maintained in leisure-time activities. The dacha allocated to Mikhail was, in keeping with his position as First Secretary of the City Komsomol Committee, noticeably more modest than those of the party cadres. The Gorbachevs managed, however, to take over more comfortably furnished dachas at reasonably short intervals, as Mikhail continued to achieve regular promotions in his professional career.

At the end of fifteen years back in his native region of Stavropol, Mikhail Gorbachev had reached the highest grade of the provincial career structure. He had become First Secretary of the Regional Committee of the Soviet Communist Party. He was therefore top man in a region whose geographical area corresponded roughly with that of the Benelux countries. While his

Stavropol position cannot, of course, be compared in terms of authority and power with the post of General Secretary in Moscow, the command structure is comparable, as it was modelled on the Moscow pattern. The First Secretary of a region is absolute ruler of his territory. Nothing can be carried out without his consent, and nothing escapes his authority. He is financially accountable only to the Moscow leadership. He is Moscow's executive manager in the region. But regional affairs are managed in the knowledge that Moscow is far away, making it impossible to check on every detail. I must state categorically here and now that no one has ever given the slightest hint that there was any abuse of his authority in Stavropol by Mikhail Gorbachev. It is universally accepted that he was already carrying out his official duties with the integrity that has so clearly stamped his leadership at the highest level in Moscow. Far more emphatically than his predecessors, Mikhail Gorbachev used his talents for the good of the people. He found in Stavropol opportunities for experiment which prepared him for operating on a larger scale in Moscow. At the same time, it must be remembered that he had the formidable handicap of having to work within the doctrinal structure of a totalitarian regime. He could attack corruption and the acceptance of bribes, but he could not break down the inflexible Soviet system in Stavropol any more than he has so far succeeded in doing in Moscow.

Mikhail Gorbachev's progress to power in Stavropol was also that of his wife Raisa. She became the First Lady of the region and began to set the tone for its womenfolk. She became the focus of public attention, and was, although living in a Communist society, surrounded by sycophants, who were looking for personal favours from their association with the family of the First Secretary. There was within the Soviet Union at that time, especially among party activists, a drive towards material affluence. People pressured the party leadership, seeking favours or actual protection. These endeavours made a particular impact since they were made during a period of reappraisal, when Russia was having to come to terms with the cost of Stalin and his dictatorship. For years Stalin had preached self-denial. The years of the Great Patriotic War had been harsh, a time of deprivation. Now with the war and Stalin part of history, the vast majority of party officials were demanding their share of the national cake, even if it was not yet completely baked. In the Brezhnev era (1964–82) the tendency among the governing class to grab things for themselves was encouraged and developed, with the result that corruption engulfed the Soviet Union at unbelievable speed.

Although it was plainly impossible under the existing system to lead the general population into lush pastures, that did not stop ordinary people from wanting a taste of paradise for themselves. The extreme poverty of large sections of the Russian people existed in glaring contrast to the prosperous conditions enjoyed by the party hegemony, whose immediate supporters were organized along Mafia 'family' lines to ensure its continuance.

Mikhail Gorbachev belonged to the generation of 'regional overlords' who came to positions of authority in the Brezhnev years. It needed a strong character to resist the temptations of power under such conditions. If communism actually meant equality for everyone, then a party man had to demonstrate this by example; he must claim for himself only such things as he was ready to grant to others. The Gorbachev family had to live continuously under the stress of this political situation, and pressure was exerted on Raisa. Offers were made to her almost daily. Acceptance would have made her relatively easy life even more comfortable, but it would have meant involvement with bribery and corruption. It cannot be claimed with cast-iron certainty that Raisa did not accept any presents or help in any way to protect her husband's position. At the same time, it must be said that contemporaries of the Gorbachevs are unanimous in pronouncing them clear of any taint of corruption. They are regarded as not just white, but whiter than white. If there were any specks of scandal, they were small and insignificant.

The character of a person does not change overnight. Without discounting the repressive methods used in the USSR until recently to sanitize official biographies, I am perfectly ready to believe a Gorbachev anecdote given to me in the course of my research for this book. In Pyatigorsk, a middle-sized town not far from Stavropol, there is a factory renowned for its delicious cakes and pastries. It was the custom of the factory director to take a fine assortment of chocolate and confectionery at regular intervals to the First Secretary of the region for him to taste. It was in reality a mild bribe. Gorbachev is said to have returned the assortment to the factory each time, and wished them 'Bon appetit' as they tasted their own products.

The Gorbachevs may have preferred to refuse such gifts, but they did not renounce the comfortable life that went with the job of 'regional overlord'. Mikhail Gorbachev's predecessors had ensured that the basis for a life free from material problems had been well established.

The family moved from their former apartment, which had given them only 200 square metres of living space, to a roomy, two-storey townhouse in a quiet street in the centre of Stavropol. Brick, with stucco render, the house was painted in the bright colours traditional in southern Russia. The ground floor comprised reception rooms, the dining room, a pantry and kitchen. The first floor was taken up by bedrooms, Mikhail Gorbachev's study and the library. The modest-sized garden around the house was filled with flowers.

At the beginning of the 1970s shops were opened throughout the Soviet Union to cater exclusively for nomenklatura families. They were permitted to buy imported goods such as clothes, shoes, household consumer goods, television and stereo equipment at prices subsidized by the state. Stavropol provides a measure of the small number of customers eligible to use these shops. Out of a population of more than 100,000, the figure was not above 100. The range of merchandise on sale in these 'cadre shops' gradually widened considerably, a fact which can almost certainly be linked with the increased foreign currency available to the Soviet Union in the 1970s through its exports of natural oil and gas to the West. The acceptance of Western goods in exchange for Soviet produce, through a kind of barter system, also helped to stock the shelves of the 'cadre shops' with merchandise from the West.

More than half of these coveted consumer items came from Finland, for the Finns had soon realized that in Soviet Russia they had a market for goods they could not export elsewhere. Finnish clothes are comfortable and practical, sometimes of good quality, but, with the exception of coats and jackets, scarcely any Finnish-made clothes follow Western fashion trends. Dresses, suits and shoes in provincial styles were exported to the Soviet Union. The dresses were often made of synthetic fabric, which meant they were unsuitable for the climate of the southern USSR. Despite this, the demand for Finnish products remained keen. It was a ruling-class status symbol to dress ostentatiously in imported clothes not available to ordinary Russians.

The supply and distribution of everyday household necessities also improved for the nomenklatura during this period. Until the beginning of the 1970s, it was still routine for domestic servants or the housewife herself to shop for food, fruit and vegetables in government shops or in the free market. A new category of 'cadre shops' to cater for these items was introduced, one to which the rest of the population was of course not admitted. In rural areas food-producing factories were developed for the purpose of supplying the 'closed shops' exclusively. Prices charged in the special shops were, as a rule, far from realistic. A pound of sirloin beef, for instance, cost only a twentieth of the amount charged in an ordinary shop; in any case, it was almost impossible for the general Russian public to buy meat of this quality. Fruit and vegetables, too, were on sale at one tenth of the market price. All these arrangements enabled the nomenklatura, from the Central Bureau in Moscow to the remotest regional headquarters, to build up a well-organized shopping system, providing them with the good life.

Mikhail Sergeyevich Gorbachev's promotion to First Secretary of the Stavropol Regional Committee entitled him and his family to a superior class of medical treatment. The No. 4 Administrative Department of the Ministry of Health in the Soviet Union became responsible for their welfare. This is the department supervising the health care of the most senior party officials, members of the Central Committee, ministers, the highest-ranking armed forces officers, members and candidates for the Politburo. Among provincial cadres, only First Secretaries of District and Regional Party Committees receive this preferential medical treatment. They belong by virtue of their office to the Central Committee of the party. Mikhail, Raisa and their daughter Irina would receive an annual comprehensive medical examination in the Central Clinic of the 4th Administrative Department in Rublev Street, Moscow, which had facilities for treating serious health problems as well as minor matters such as spectacle frames for Mikhail Gorbachev.

Treatment in the Central Clinic was associated with another major privilege. The hospital had access to a wide-ranging network of convalescent homes and sanatoria stretching right across the Soviet Union, from the south coast of the Black Sea to the northernmost regions of Russia. In the Brezhnev years health centres proliferated. New ones were always under construction. Central Clinic clients generally preferred the older establishments, built in the time of Stalin or earlier, decorated with marble and coloured brickwork, and, perhaps more importantly, located in the south of the country.

The Gorbachevs were able in the early 1970s to spend their leave for the first time in the select health resort of Oreanda in the Crimea, one which is reserved for officials of the highest rank, and which still exists today. It is a palatial forestry building of bright yellow and rose-coloured brick. The wide verandah looking out on to the lawn and the balconies of the rooms are all paved with marble. Southern roses in overhanging stone bowls are in bloom everywhere. In spite of the summer heat the rooms are shady and cool. Brick paths in the southern park of the Oreanda are covered in fine, dark shingle and lead down to the beach.

The finest landscape architects in Russia have been deployed to create an idyllic and splendid setting. Streams wind across the garden; on their banks are summerhouses garlanded with vines. One enclosed beach is for sunbathing, and has little huts to protect guests from the high summer heat. In contrast to the beaches in Yalta or Sochi, where ordinary Russian citizens can take a holiday, the beach at Oreanda is spotlessly clean. It looks as if every pebble has been washed with soap and carefully replaced in its exact position. The beach café serves refreshing herbal tea, and, on request, a 'Kremlin cookie', a delicious yeasty bun.

The sanatorium itself is equipped on the most up-to-date medical lines. Only highly qualified doctors, nurses, masseurs and physiotherapists are on the staff. Long walks are carefully marked out along the paths in the grounds so that each resident can take the exercise prescribed by the doctor. The cuisine is traditionally gourmet, with some twenty-five variants of an entire menu, any of which can be ordered according to personal preference or in consultation with a sanatorium dietitian.

The Gorbachevs usually spent four weeks in the luxurious atmosphere of Oreanda, which gave them, as well as a holiday, the chance to undergo any necessary medical treatment. They were frequent visitors to Oreanda, its setting obviously appealing to their taste.

Nor were holiday options for the newly-appointed First Secretary of the Regional Committee of Stavropol confined to the best spas and sanatoria in his own country. Important provincial party officials were increasingly given the opportunity by Moscow to spend their leaves in the homes of Western Communist parties. Not long after Gorbachev had taken over his senior post in Stavropol, the Gorbachevs were allowed to spend a few weeks of their leave in one of the sanatoria belonging to the Italian Communist party on the Mediterranean.

This arrangement is still in force. Party officials from Moscow are regular guests in the holiday homes of Western Communists. Security considerations, however, can restrict the foreign holiday opportunities of top Kremlin officials. Unless there is some urgent medical reason, a secretary of the Central Committee or a Politburo member is forbidden to take his leave in a non-Communist country. They can spend their vacations only in the secure residences of eastern bloc comrades. Holiday homes in the Thuringian forest of East Germany were particularly popular with the Moscow cadres. Precisely why Thuringia was preferred is not easy to say, but one possible reason may have been that particularly desirable 'merchandise' could be brought back from a leave spent in East Germany, long regarded as the 'consumers paradise' of the eastern bloc. Comrades in East Germany were also said to go to more trouble than those in other Communist countries to please their guests from Moscow.

For Raisa, the many advantages of life as the First Lady of a large region did not compensate for its many drawbacks. Life at the top of the Soviet provincial hierarchy led inexorably to the strict isolation which Brezhnev imposed on all his senior party officials. The array of privileges that the nomenklatura enjoyed must under no circumstances become known outside the closed circle. The separation of the governing group from the governed was, through this secrecy, effectively achieved.

In their period as First Family of a large Soviet region, the Gorbachevs too distanced themselves from the mundane realities of life. What they said counted, and people around them paid attention to what they did. Nobody dared to make any serious criticism of the First Secretary. There were, inevitably, all kinds of rumours, with Raisa herself as the prime target for gossip. These were circumstances to which the Gorbachevs had to adjust, and Raisa reacted in the only sensible way open to her; she concentrated on her family, shrugging off petty gossip, of which she was nevertheless aware. She unlocked her social isolation by defining her own fields of activity. She took an informed and intense interest in the arts. In doing so she was fulfilling an ambition she had nourished since her student days in Moscow.

Raisa was specially attracted to the theatre. She not only attended all the first nights in Stavropol; she met theatre managers and actors for regular conferences on future programmes, where they discussed current productions and put up ideas for possible plays. Her extensive knowledge not merely of Russian and Soviet literature but of drama world-wide made her advice worth having. Not all her suggestions were accepted, sometimes because the local players were not equal to them. Stavropol was an outpost of Russian theatre that could not attract the most talented actors or the best directors. The most gifted and experienced theatre people looked for work in Moscow, Leningrad, Kiev or the capital cities of the Asiatic republics, cultural centres where imaginative artistic ideas had some chance of recognition. Stavropol was still handicapped by its conservatism and lack of any regional cultural tradition. This was only too evident in the tastes of its citizens. Audiences much preferred a second-rate soap opera or an uninspired drama about the Revolution to the great Russian plays, whether classical or avant-garde.

Still, Raisa would not be turned aside from her intention of reclaiming the cultural wasteland of Stavropol. She eventually succeeded in attracting, if only for guest performances, Russian artists with national names to the provincial city, and in mounting exhibitions – in short, in establishing a basis for cultural activity. It is hard to judge whether her efforts have had a lasting effect, but it can be said unequivocally that during the time she was at the centre of things attendances at theatres and concerts went up.

While she was First Lady of Stavropol Raisa also turned her attention to the education of the rural population. The active research she had undertaken in the villages of the Stavropol region in preparation for her doctoral thesis in sociology had made her aware of the horrifying educational backwardness of the people. The main city of Stavropol could hardly be called a cultural oasis, but once you travelled outside the city boundaries, social and cultural amenities disappeared at breathtaking speed. In the mid-1960s some 40 per cent of families on collective farms had members who had never enjoyed regular education and could barely read and write. Unquestionably this illiteracy strengthened the hold that superstitious belief had on the region.

The strenuousness of an agricultural labourer's working day, which usually lasted fifteen hours, and the absence of any labour-saving machinery, meant that in rural areas leisure time was unknown. The basic condition for cultural development was lacking. If people read anything, it was a newspaper. As a rule only schoolchildren read books, those they had been set to read as part of the syllabus. Such culture and learning as country children acquired at school was soon lost once they were caught up in the unremitting grind of agricultural labour.

Raisa's first-hand experience as a sociologist convinced her that before the educational levels of agricultural workers could be raised, their living and working conditions would have to be improved. That remains true today. Rural Russia is still extremely backward, though radio and television have made country people in the Soviet Union more conscious of the world outside.

Her preliminary research also persuaded Raisa that the answer was not to fill the shelves of village libraries with books. If rural people were to become aware of the splendours of art and culture, they would, she decided, have to be *introduced* to them, in the literal sense of the word. She can look back with satisfaction on the fact that people from the region's rural areas now have regular opportunities to attend theatre, concert and variety performances in Stavropol itself. She arranged for buses or farm vehicles to bring people in from outlying districts to see the city museums, to go on excursions to places of historical interest and beauty. It cannot be said that this programme inspired a cultural revolution, but Raisa's purposeful concentration on what could be achieved in rural areas in the educational sphere is still regarded in Stavropol today as having helped to shift the region out of its torpor into a more progressive future.

Possibly Raisa's most significant achievement during those

years, and one which cannot be emphasized too strongly, was the influence she exerted on her husband. She impressed on him with utter conviction the belief that there were peaks beyond Stravropol that he could conquer.

Mikhail himself, according to some of his former Stavropol colleagues, sometimes showed a tendency to be easygoing, to rest content with his achievements. He had in a comparatively short time gained promotions within the party for which most officials might spend a lifetime vainly struggling. Raisa, though, was confident that her husband had particular qualities and depths that set him apart from the usual run of provincial administrators. He was intelligent, approachable and, above all, impervious to the corruption of authoritative power. I don't think one should assume that Raisa's encouragement of her husband to pursue ever larger ambitions means that her eyes were always fixed on a return to Moscow. Given the power structure of the Communist party, it is simply not credible that from the beginning she envisaged her husband sitting in the Kremlin as General Secretary. The fact remains that she undoubtedly inspired Mikhail never to rest happy with his latest promotion, but to continue to look restlessly for fresh victories.

Raisa devoted her full energy and intelligence to helping her husband in his career. She spent her free time summarizing not just technical books that gave him useful factual information, but works of art and literature, to stimulate his mental and spiritual imagination. Her academic background enabled her to prepare well-researched papers for him on many subjects. What must have been immeasurably valuable to the First Secretary were their private discussions at home, when he could advance opinions without any ideological or bureaucratic constraint. That gave him support for the tasks of the day. Raisa's role as 'intellectual sparring partner' in discussion and researcher of information is one she still plays to this day.

The observant reader will of course question Raisa's motives in all this. They may well be mixed, and it would, in my view, need a psychoanalytical report to fathom them. What I believe is that Raisa had the intelligence to perceive, well ahead of other nomenklatura wives, that political changes in the Soviet Union opened up remarkable opportunities for a bold reformer. Such a man would have to stretch his capacities to the uttermost, and expose the nepotism and corruption undermining society in the USSR.

Even if today she minimizes her role behind the scenes, she would not be a woman if she had not sometimes dreamed in faraway Stavropol of life at the top.

4

Dr Raisa Gorbachev

Nancy Reagan, wife of the former American President, made
what was for her a truly remarkable discovery. During her
briefing for her first encounter with Raisa Gorbachev, US State
Department protocol staff told her that the Russian language has
no equivalent expression for Mrs Reagan's own title of 'First
Lady'. Information officers emphasized to her that a woman's
role in the Soviet Union bears no comparison with that of an
American woman. In the USSR, some seventy years after the
Revolution, certain ways of thought and behaviour have not
changed since the days of the tsars, when a woman was expected
to be subordinate to her husband in every respect. Nancy Reagan
was told that it was far from unusual to find Soviet women
working in mining and road-building, and lifting heavy weights.
When Mrs Reagan was shown films and photographs which
proved this, she was said to have been greatly impressed. She
could hardly believe that such dramatic contrasts could exist
between two civilized countries.

President Reagan had declared not long before his first summit
meeting with the Soviet leader that their country was 'an evil
Empire'. Reagan, his defence advisers and other senior members
of the US administration had talked openly about 'bombing the
Soviet Union back into the Stone Age'. Hardly a day passed
without the publication of some new threatening scenario in the
newspapers of the world. At a personal level, however, Nancy
Reagan could not get a clear picture of the Soviet woman whom
she was to partner for several days of a programme jointly

designed for her and Raisa, and with whom she would be endlessly photographed, alongside their husbands.

Who is Raisa Gorbachev, the woman who disembarks from the official Soviet airliner alongside her husband on overseas trips, but on their return to Moscow avoids the spotlight, discreetly following the baggage porters from the aircraft? She seems self-confident, is highly educated, with a PhD. Reports from London said that on an early visit to the UK before her husband was chosen for the highest office in the Soviet Union, she astonished journalists and her political hosts by her command of English. Practically nothing had been known abroad about the previous head of the Kremlim, Konstantin Chernenko, or his predecessor, Yuri Andropov, not even whether he was married or not. It was only when a grieving woman was shown on television standing beside Andropov's coffin, with Gorbachev endeavouring to comfort her, that people realized that this was the wife of the deceased Kremlin leader.

The modern, progressive style that Gorbachev imposed on the Soviet Union involved the wife of the Russian leader in a new role; she had to appear – at least in foreign countries – as the First Lady of the USSR, even though she was not officially authorized to do so at home. Certainly Raisa knows how to attract public attention. Nothing about her can possibly remind people of Khrushchev's clumsy, awkward wife, Nina, who at the Vienna summit meeting in 1961 looked almost like a charwoman standing next to the elegant Jackie Kennedy, and not simply because she was dressed in unfashionable clothes. Nina Khrushchev never appeared at ease with the part in public life that her position as wife of the Soviet leader required of her.

In contrast, Raisa never invites the faintest suspicion that she has any problem in fulfilling her official role. She is self-confident, decisive. She knows exactly what she wants. Nor can one overlook the way, even in public, she uses her influence on her husband. Mikhail Gorbachev, who likes to chat informally with journalists covering an event, can sometimes be called to order by Raisa, with a 'Misha! Misha!' in her 'pay attention' voice. Raisa's self-confidence stems partly, without question , from her academic brilliance. Throughout her educational career, as I have said, she consistently gained the highest possible marks in her examinations. Although the Soviet academic system differs in many respects from the Western one, in both cases a student achieves outstanding results only through scholastic merit. In ideological subjects such as philosophy and sociology, other factors may well, in a Communist country, come into consideration. The fact that as soon as Raisa had graduated from Moscow University she was offered the chance to begin her doctorate indicates that her academic level was well above that of the average student.

A huge set of bookshelves, filled with volumes from world literature, bound in leather or cloth. Individual editions, collected works of famous writers. Everything beautifully arranged. Raisa stands in front of the shelves, studying the rows of books with an informed eye. Within seconds she confidently picks out a book. The photograph on my desk, which I am looking at as I write, leaves no doubt that Raisa is intellectually at ease with books. One feels she is a woman for whom books are a necessity of life. Even the way she looks at them confirms the impression that her approach to books is scholarly.

Until the Gorbachevs moved to Moscow in 1978, Raisa had a job in the Department of Philosophy at the Stavropol Agricultural Institute. The reason why she was working at this educational establishment rather than at one of the other three colleges in the city was a logical decision by the Moscow cadre committee. When Mikhail Gorbachev was selected for his appointment in Stavropol, Raisa had a choice: she could either continue to study for her doctorate in Moscow, which would entail separation from her husband, or she could try to find a professional post in Stavropol. Raisa opted to accompany her husband.

Her first task at the Agricultural Institute was to take seminars based on the philosophy lectures. An unrewarding assignment, since the students, who were at college primarily to study agriculture, saw Raisa's subject as compulsory but irrelevant. Of course no student objected openly to the philosophy course. None dared to ask whether the cereal crop of a future farmer would grow better if he had some acquaintance with philosophy than if he hadn't, or whether the hens of the future manageress of a poultry farm would lay more perfect eggs for someone well-qualified in Marxism-Leninism than for an ignorant old farmer's wife. Russians did not ask that sort of question at this period.

Professor Mikhail Pankratovich Chuguyev, a colleague of

Raisa at this time and still on friendly terms with her, can remember the wife of the head of the Kremlin when she was a university teacher. 'Although Raisa Maximovna had no experience as a teacher, she was so self-possessed in the lecture room that she gave you the impression that she had taught all her life. Inspectors used to sit in on lectures at the Institute quite often, though I cannot recall exactly why they did so. Raisa always asked that her teaching methods should be assessed by the inspectors as a matter of priority. She was remarkably cool and self-assured. Not that she was arrogant, rather that she felt secure in her professional expertise. In the course of my academic career I can't remember one member of staff who did not sometimes have an off day, or occasionally come to lectures or seminars unprepared. However hard I search my memory, I must confess that Raisa was an exception to this rule. Please don't imagine that I am singling out my former colleague for special praise just because her husband is now General Secretary of the Soviet Communist Party. You simply must not believe that. Raisa was always very conscientious and ambitious. And another thing: almost without exception, the women students who finished college with a gold medal had attended her courses. They reached a significantly higher level of academic attainment than the other students. Although Raisa's attitude to her pupils was demanding, she enjoyed not just their respect but that of her colleagues on the teaching staff.'

Professor Chuguyev stressed that his glowing assessment of his former colleague had nothing to do with her husband's present eminence. It is nevertheless difficult to accept his effusive recollections without reserve. Raisa's critics often pick on the slow, deliberate manner of speech she uses on public occasions. The manner is almost certainly a legacy of the classroom. Teachers everywhere are trained to speak slowly and emphatically, making Raisa's manner of speech something she shares not just with Soviet teachers, but teachers worldwide. Nearly twenty-two years of teaching would leave their mark on anybody, and it may well be one of the less attractive characteristics that Raisa has carried over from her profession into everyday life.

As she became more experienced, Raisa began to give lectures herself. Students and colleagues recall her ability to be interesting about a wide range of topics, saying she could present the most abstruse subjects in straightforward, comprehensible language.

She used concrete examples to provide flashes of insight, illuminating even such potentially arid subjects as ethics and aesthetics, in which she specialized. Raisa possessed another quality as a teacher which her pupils may not always have appreciated. She scrupulously followed their progress throughout the academic year, sometimes for their entire college careers. If she became convinced that any of her pupils was for some reason or other not giving their full attention to their studies, she could be really angry with them. She demanded that Stavropol's future farmers should study philosophy and related subjects as diligently as they studied agriculture. In spite of the fulsome praise given now to Raisa as a teacher, when she was active in the profession her tendency to be a stickler for principle actually provoked some argument and criticism from students and colleagues. But as the wife of Mikhail Sergeyevich Gorbachev, an important party official, she was not criticized in public.

Raisa's immunity from *public* criticism in Stavropol's academic circles was reinforced when people saw her arrive as a passenger in her husband's personal staff car, which duly took her to college and brought her home at the end of the college day. In the final years of her stay in Stavropol she was escorted everywhere by one of her husband's bodyguards, specifically detailed by Mikhail Gorbachev to look after her personal protection.

The official duties which Mikhail Gorbachev carried out as first Secretary of a regional Committee of the Soviet Communist Party are reasonably similar to those of an American state governor. Police bodyguards are assigned to such political VIPs not only for their own personal protection; they are extended to members of their families during serious political disturbances. In the Brezhnev era, which encompassed the Gorbachevs' time in Stavropol, the personal bodyguard was primarily a status symbol, advertising one's power and importance. I know of no instance of a direct threat of violence to a Soviet provincial politician or party official, and while, admittedly, some events in recent Soviet history may well remain hidden today, the evidence suggests that in the present liberalized climate little that previously happened in the Soviet Union has not now been uncovered.

Raisa talked about personal matters only to her closest friends. There was, in fact, nothing sensational to tell. The few close women friends she had were impressed by how well the Gorbachevs got along together. Among strangers, who would include most of her colleagues at the Agricultural Institute and certainly all the students, she was extremely discreet, discussing with them only questions and problems directly concerned with her teaching and their work. This reserve seemed at first sight to present me as her biographer with an almost insurmountable difficulty. How could I hope to give an objective description of the life of someone who adamantly refused to be interviewed? However, gradually and over a period, I managed to solve most of the problems, or at least the major ones, created by her reserve.

Eventually I assembled a significantly larger number of photographs than I had thought possible at the beginning of my research. When I examined these photographs at leisure, I realized that although I had extensive coverage of most phases of Raisa Gorbachev's life, I had virtually nothing to illustrate her work as a college lecturer from 1956 to 1978. No pictures of Raisa surrounded by a group of students, none of her giving a lecture or conducting a seminar. Had I come across a period in her life that had been retrospectively altered, a period that had – for whatever reason – been systematically censored? Professor Chuguyev was able to put me right. He said it had been one of Raisa's idiosyncrasies never to let herself be photographed with the students. If she went to a student's farewell party, which she seldom did, she arrived invariably after the group photographs had been taken. The reason for this? ' She always said she did not come out well in photographs,' said Professor Chuguyev.

Professor Chuguyev is quite informative about the days when Raisa Gorbachev was lecturing at the Stavropol Agricultural Institute. 'The academic staff used to celebrate birthdays and social occasions in a modest way,' he says. 'Nobody went to great expense for a party. Usually members of staff gathered in a lecture room, pushed the chairs together, drank tea and ate cakes. I can remember that once on her birthday Raisa brought a little bottle of brandy with her, which in itself was something out of the ordinary, for as a rule Raisa does not touch alcohol.' He added with a sly smile: 'It was the depth of winter in Stavropol, and most of the staff were more than keen to warm the inner man.'

Professor Chuguyev took me on a personal tour of the lecture halls and seminar rooms where Raisa worked. He showed me visual aids, newspaper cuttings, plans and sketches, which, he said, Raisa had prepared. From the dates of the newspaper cuttings, already yellowing with age, what he said was possibly true, but I was not entirely convinced. When Professor Chuguyev caught the look of doubt on my face, he reacted in a way I had not expected. Did I take him for a liar? I endeavoured to pacify him but the one hint of scepticism I had shown meant that the old professor watched me defensively as he made every subsequent comment. Every other sentence he would snap curtly: 'That is the truth!' He showed me a writing-table, at which, he said, Raisa had sat and worked. Students are sometimes led to this spot and reminded of who wrote there. 'Sit here,' they are told, 'and perhaps one day you too will achieve something great.'

'Raisa generally avoided controversy,' Professor Chuguyev said, resuming his reminiscences over a glass of Russian tea. 'She disliked squabbles and arguments. When they did happen, she always kept her cool and good manners. I remember one occasion when even she lost her temper. It must have been in the mid-1970s. The college introduced the somewhat humiliating practice of making secret recordings of lectures, which were later evaluated by the governing body. Nobody liked the system, but everyone kept quiet, because they did not want to antagonize the college principal. When Raisa Gorbachev discovered that her lectures, too, had been secretly recorded, she was appalled. Part of her was deeply disillusioned, part furiously angry. She went straight to the Dean to complain about this unlawful procedure, and, I may add, none of this took place discreetly. The Dean tried to justify himself by pleading the existence of ministerial authorization for the secret recording of lectures. Raisa did not believe him and wanted more precise information about this ruling, which she saw only as an insult to academic staff. Of course, the Dean could produce nothing in writing, for there was no such authorization. Following his confrontation with Raisa the unauthorized practice of recording lectures in secret came abruptly to an end.'

In Stavropol I also met Ekaterina Grigorievna Dsybal, another colleague of Raisa's at the Agricultural Institute. When I said I was interested in Raisa as a lecturer she reacted immediately: 'It was not unusual for wives of senior party officials to work at the Institute. Some soon let it be known that they considered themselves superior to us, not just by their general attitude but also in the way they dressed. You know, when a woman changes her outfit several times in a day, that in itself comes across as quite a put-down for another woman with only a couple of dresses in her wardrobe. Raisa was not condescending, like some of the wives, though I can imagine she probably had as many different outfits as they had. At college Raisa never dressed conspicuously, though this changed considerably later on, when her husband became General Secretary of the party. As a lecturer she almost always wore the same outfit, almost a uniform, a black suit and a white blouse. In winter her favourite clothes were an orange-coloured mohair sweater and a simply-cut black coat. The coat came from one of the shops 'for officials only' in Stavropol, but she had brought the pullover back from Italy, when she went with her husband in 1972 to a celebration arranged by an Italian Communist newspaper.'

Ekaterina added: 'Raisa used hardly any make-up, just a touch of lipstick, which she put on unobtrusively – far less garishly than most Russian women – and she never gave herself airs. Neither was she very outgoing, but reserve is part of her nature; it was not expressive of her attitude to us in particular.'

She recalled what happened when Mikhail Gorbachev was made First Secretary of the Stavropol Regional Committee in 1970. 'Raisa said to us: "Comrades, I have a large favour to ask you. Would you please not come to me with personal requests, appeals and problems, in the hope that I can put them before my husband. I have no right to try and influence him. So please don't place me in an awkward position." She made the situation clear to us once and for all, and so far as I know none of her colleagues tried to obtain advantages through Raisa that her husband could have provided.'

I think I ought to explain here something of the relevant background to life in the Soviet Union at the time. For a Soviet citizen, connections with a high-ranking party official or somebody close to him might not be a matter of life or death, but could be the key to a whole range of possibilities in everyday life. Somebody with 'connections' experienced no bottlenecks in supplies and didn't always have to stand at the end of a long queue in order to obtain basic daily necessities. How did you acquire these connections? If you did not belong to a specific group or to the extended family of a senior party official, you could try to build up or promote connections by doing favours; you could go so far as to become an informer. Necessity is often the mother of invention.

Raisa set out from the beginning to avoid too-close relationships with people outside her immediate family circle. That way she escaped entanglement in a network of favours given and received; she remained free of obligations. She was not vulnerable to flatterers and sycophants. Her few genuine friends were carefully chosen. Nor did Raisa claim any special privileges for herself. I kept coming across evidence of her punctiliousness in keeping to the rules. For instance, when her husband was travelling to Moscow for the Twenty-Fourth Party Congress Raisa was invited to accompany him, and the chance of three days in Moscow would have meant a great deal to her. Most working wives of party officials would, in a similar situation, have simply informed their superiors that they would not be available for work for a few days. Raisa, however, chose to go through the proper channels. She asked the college Dean for an appointment to obtain from him official leave of absence from work for her visit to Moscow. She could have ensured that the hours of duty she missed were simply written off, but characteristically, she insisted on making up all her lost time. Even when her daughter Irina was ill, Raisa did not expect any favours, again making up the hours that were lost nursing her daughter. Nowadays some might observe cynically that her scruples were exaggerated. She is plainly no ordinary woman. But Raisa's attitude contains a truth which helps to keep her beyond criticism. The abuse of privileges which accompany high office has caused the foundering of so many political careers, not just in the Soviet Union.

Let us return to Ekaterina Grigorievna Dysbal, who had a flow of anecdotes about her former colleague: one a harmless April Fool's Day joke played on Raisa, the other a cruel hoax.

'It was April 1st and Raisa was waiting anxiously for a response from the editor of a learned journal to an article she had submitted. For some reason or other the reply was delayed. Some of us from the Institute went to the Post Office with an envelope and persuaded one of the officials there to frank it. As you know, every scholar likes to see his or her work in print. Inside the envelope was a letter we had written, in which the editor allegedly stated that the article had been well liked and was going to be published. In addition he expressed the hope that the author of such an outstanding article should give an account of her researches to an international academic conference in Moscow. We quietly put the letter on her desk and watched for her reaction. Raisa was overjoyed. "Comrades, my article has been accepted. Let's celebrate!" she said. We could restrain ourselves no longer. We all burst out laughing, and Raisa realized that we had dared to make fun of her. But she wasn't a spoilsport and joined in the laughter.

'Another trick played on her was callous in the extreme. It must have happened early in the 1970s, for Mikhail Sergeyevich Gorbachev was already First Secretary of the Regional Party Committee. In the middle of a lecture Raisa was suddenly summoned to the telephone. I saw her turn pale and sink into a chair. The caller had told her that her husband had been killed in a car accident. People shouldn't joke about things like that. But anybody could be the victim of that kind of cruel hoax.'

Although Raisa's ability as a lecturer at the Agricultural College was generally recognized, it is probable, given the social climate of the time that it was primarily her husband's status that induced the governing body of the Institute to promote her to be Professor of Philosophy. Raisa herself believed initially that the appointment was an acknowledgement of her academic and teaching achievements. She was delighted by the promotion. Within a month she saw through the governing body's manoeuvre, realizing they had been thinking not about the academic career of an able woman but about the power in the hands of her husband. Raisa reacted swiftly and informed the Dean that she wished to relinquish the chair. It was unprecedented at the time for someone to give up a major academic post voluntarily, with no pressure from outside. No one was able to talk Raisa out of her decision. She saw her selection for the professorship as a form of humiliation and she could not endure it. She told her astonished colleagues succinctly that she did not much like administrative work and, in addition, she was not personally set on an academic career anyway.

Shortly after Raisa joined the staff of the Stavropol Agricultural Institute, she had begun research into a specific project, the living conditions of peasants in rural areas. The Stavropol region had many natural advantages for farming development, but in one respect it was no different from other rural regions in the Soviet Union: the living conditions of people working on the land were worse than wretched. The political leadership in Stavropol seems to have recognized earlier than administrators in other regions that increased agricultural production hinged on an improvement in the living and working conditions of farm labourers. What was required was a trustworthy report on the actual situation prepared by someone with qualifications in sociology. Raisa was selected for the task.

The project appealed immediately to the young academic, who had been studying sociological subjects while still at Moscow University. Her husband was also keen for her to undertake the research. He was responsible for agriculture, as for so many official aspects of life in Stavropol. There has been much speculation in the Western media as to why Mikhail Gorbachev tends to make a large number of his decisions on sociological grounds, in a way his predecessors never did. One good reason may well be that his wife has convinced him that sociology is a vital factor in political management. She argued most insistently that politics cannot be simply a matter of spontaneous action, however inspired, but must rest on objectively researched information. The reality is that although Gorbachev has striven to follow his wife's undeniably sound advice, four years of *glasnost* and *perestroika* have not yet been enough to compensate for seventy years of maladministration.

While she was doing her sociological research in Stavropol, Raisa decided to resume work on the doctorate in sociology she had begun while at Moscow University. It was not possible for a college in Stavropol to supervise her studies. Sociology as an academic discipline was still in the process of freeing itself from the distortions of the Stalin era. The Lenin Pedagogical Institute in Moscow was at this time reckoned the most progressive, so it seemed logical to Raisa to prepare her dissertation under their supervision. While she was still a lecturer in Stavropol she travelled to Moscow several times a year, took part in various academic functions, produced the findings of her research and discussed these with leading social scientists.

During these trips to Moscow, Raisa got to know the Professor of Philosophy at the Pedagogical Institute, Professor Vladimir

Spiridonovich Gott, whom she still regards as one of her most valued mentors. A man of about eighty, he still spends several weeks every summer with the Gorbachevs in their dacha at Pitsunda on the Black Sea, in itself a proof of friendship, for few people are admitted to the Gorbachevs' intimate circle. Gott has lived a life with a variety of experiences. He had a high academic reputation as a specialist in the philosophy of natural science. The Stalin regime made use of him early on for their own purposes. Gott soon became one of the most trusted colleagues of Vyacheslav Molotov, Stalin's Foreign Minister, taking part in some of Molotov's most important meetings and negotiations. The information that Raisa's doctoral supervisor, Gennady Osipov, gave me about this long-time confidant of the Gorbachevs is indirectly sensational. Gott has in his possession a copy of the Hitler–Stalin Pact. He is one of the few remaining living witnesses to the event, and could clear up much of the mystery still surrounding the treaty, such as its secret codicil, in which Hitler and Stalin agreed on the way eastern Europe would be carved up into their spheres of influence. The professor, however, keeps his counsel, refusing to make his private information public. In addition to the Hitler–Stalin document, Gott possesses a copy of Molotov's will, which gives the background to some of the most significant aspects of Stalin's foreign policy. All my efforts to see these papers and interview him met with a decisive 'Nyet' that brooked no argument. His only comment: That was a bad chapter in the history of the Soviet Union, and the Gorbachev family should not be linked with it.

Molotov's expulsion from the Presidium in 1957 affected Gott, one of his advisers, who was, however, sufficiently young and intelligent to ensure that not all Soviet doors were closed to him. Within a few years he returned to Russian academic life, and at the beginning of the 1960s was appointed Professor of Philosophy at the Lenin Pedagogical Institute. From 1965 to 1967 he personally supervised Raisa Gorbachev's studies for her doctorate, and in his capacity as chairman of the academic council he headed the committee which had to decide whether her dissertation should be accepted. Despite his great age he has not retired from academic life, remaining editor-in-chief of the learned magazine *Philosophy of Science* and Professor of Philosophy at the Soviet Academy of Sciences.

By 1964 Raisa was sufficiently well advanced in her doctoral studies to be accepted as a candidate for the higher degree. She passed the examinations with distinction. It only remained for her to complete her written thesis. In the Soviet Union every doctoral candidate is assigned to a senior academic who must be of a stipulated rank and status. The role of the supervisor of a doctoral candidate is more clearly defined and important in Soviet Russia than in other countries. The supervisor not only directs his pupil's academic work, he also influences his or her attitude to life, and is held accountable for the seriousness of his candidate's approach to intellectual values.

I went to interview Gennady Osipov, who was Raisa's supervisor when she was preparing her doctoral thesis, hopeful of some useful information. Gennady Osipov is widely viewed in the USSR as the 'kingpin' in the field of social science. The magazine *Sociological Research* said that under his leadership active social research had been undertaken in Soviet Russia for the first time ever. He was the academic who separated sociology from philosophy, making the study of society itself intellectually respectable in Russia. At the beginning of the 1960s he embarked on a sociological investigation of a village in Moldavia, which he resumed twenty-five years later and published as a book. Osipov is the author of a number of works fundamental to Russian sociology: *Sociology in the USSR*, *The Sociologist's Handbook* and *Marxist-Leninist Sociology*. On his initiative Soviet Russia established a Sociological Institute within the Academy of Sciences, of which he is now a member.

This was the man I found sitting at the other side of the table when I went to ask him about Raisa Gorbachev, the postgraduate student. An amiable man of about sixty, twice married, with a second wife some thirty years younger than he himself is, only a few years older than Raisa. He was ready to talk freely and in convincing detail about the status of sociology under Stalin.

'Sociology was considered a pseudo-science. We had practically no academically trained sociologists. Stalin could not totally deny the legitimacy of sociology, with its concern for the structure of society. But he forcibly confined sociology within social philosophy, which meant, in effect, that philosophy took over. Philosophy deals with the analysis of society on a purely abstract plane. Any attempt by academics to examine social phenomena

81

in concrete terms was regarded under Stalin as a divergence from Marxist-Leninism, as "ideological sabotage", part of a move to narrow social philosophy into positivism [which recognizes only positive facts and rejects metaphysical abstractions].

'To stand accused of ideological sabotage could cost a Russian his academic position,' Professor Osipov added bitterly, 'and for many it had more terrible consequences.' He was silent, thinking no doubt of the many academics Stalin sent to their death in the gulag labour camps.

'When the Stalin era came to an end, there was under Khrushchev a modest intellectual thaw, which enabled sociology to achieve some independence as a discipline. It was not a painless process. We sociologists had direct opposition from an array of philosophers who were still prisoners of Stalinist dogma. They reopened the old charges of ideological sabotage and accused us of wanting to undermine the existing foundations of socialist society through our researches. The forces of academic conservatism tried to obstruct sociologists by all manner of means, attempting to kill the profession while it was still in embryo.

'Life was especially hard for young sociologists. Quite a number gave up, some for the second time, and those who did remain in sociology knew that they had only a minimal chance of achieving their doctorate. Only ten out of a hundred postgraduate students gained their PhD in sociology, and even they could be accused of being "enemies of Marxist ideology". The opposition to sociologists lasted well into the 1960s, so that it needed some courage to take up sociology and persevere with it in spite of all these adverse conditions.'

Professor Osipov was himself the victim of a wave of powerful hostility in the 1960s. F. P. Trapesnikov, director of the Department of Higher Education in the Central Committee of the Soviet Communist Party, manoeuvred constantly to have Osipov stripped of his academic status. In one year alone Osipov received no fewer than five official reprimands, either from the party or from relevant government departments, which provided sufficient grounds for his arraignment. On the instructions of Millionchikov, Vice-President of the Academy of Science, legal proceedings were instituted against Gennady Osipov. Their only purpose was to discredit him both as an academic and as a man. The trial was actually scheduled for the People's Court in Brest

Street in Moscow, and it was only because the absurdity of the proceedings became so apparent that the charges were eventually withdrawn. Although there was no trial, Osipov was still put on a blacklist, which meant that for years he was forbidden to travel abroad and his academic activities were severely restricted.

When Raisa made up her mind to study for her PhD in sociology, she can have been under no illusions. She knew she was venturing into difficult terrain, where a hostile atmosphere would have to be met with moral courage. Her involvement with sociology might even have a damaging effect on her husband's career. In any case, her gaining a doctorate and her further professional progress were by no means assured. It did not deter her when Professor Gott decided that her supervisor should be Gennady Osipov, a man accused by his professional colleagues of 'bourgeois thinking' and treated with undisguised contempt.

Professor Osipov had earlier impressed on me that the difficulties under which Soviet sociologists worked arose from their peculiar situation of being half-legitimate and 'half in the basement'. He explained the odd expression 'half in the basement', when he took me off to visit 16B Pishchevaya Street in Moscow. The professor had not been there for more than twenty years, so it took him a bit of time to find it. It was in the basement of this building that the Department for Sociological Research used to be located, classed as a subsection of the Department of Philosophy in the Soviet Academy of Sciences. Hence the phrase, he said, that the research half of sociology was in the basement. He added that the basement was always extremely damp, and in winter there was frost on the walls.

'A science which was without official status,' he said, 'had no right to proper accommodation of its own. But the optimism and intellectual curiosity of my colleagues overcame every obstacle.'

In that same basement where he met Raisa Gorbachev for the first time, Professor Osipov recalled for me his first impressions of her. He had described to her frankly the problems she would face if she embarked on a PhD in sociology, but he soon realized that she was not going to be deterred. She was a young woman who had reached a decision and would stick by it. He was impressed. There was nothing superficial about her enthusiasm; she was practical and determined.

'I think that from the beginning,' he said, 'I sensed that the underlying motive for her commitment to sociology was to equip herself to support her husband in his career.' He could not have known at that first interview that sociology was an interest Raisa shared with Mikhail Gorbachev.

Once she began her advanced studies, Raisa visited Moscow regularly, meeting her supervisor, Professor Osipov, in the damp basement rooms in Pishchevaya Street, presenting her interim findings and outlining her general thesis for his observations. Mikhail Gorbachev sometimes accompanied his wife, and the casual conversation with Osipov and Raisa usually moved to a serious level, as they discussed the questions Raisa would deal with in her dissertation. Gorbachev broadened these discussions by his practical knowledge and experience of conditions on collective farms, which had convinced him that reforms were needed urgently. The visible indication that Gorbachev was in Moscow was his black Volga staff car, parked outside the building in Pishchevaya Street, where in the researchers' basement Raisa and Professor Osipov were discussing her work.

I am most grateful to Professor Osipov not only for enabling me to become the first Western journalist to have access to Raisa Gorbachev's finished thesis, but also for providing me with the relevant background.

A few days after our first meeting, he allowed me to see the first thesis ever written by the wife of a head of the Kremlin, which I began to read in translation. Academic dissertations in the Soviet Union, as everywhere else, are given long-winded titles. This one was called; *On the Formation of a New Pattern of Life for the Kolkhoz Peasantry, Based on Material Obtained through Sociological Research in the Stavropol Region.* Raisa Gorbachev set out its main objectives as finding the answer to these questions:

> What are the fundamental features and tendencies underlying the development of living conditions on collective farms?
> What are the problems and obstacles that prevent the development of improved conditions for collective farm workers?
> How can solutions be found to these problems?
> What influence do the particular socio-economic circumstances of the collective farm system have on the daily lives of workers and their families?

I must confess that I found the questions at first glance a bit irksome. I had to consider how this academic material was going to fit in with a biography of Raisa Gorbachev intended for the general reader, but had also to remember that I would be publishing extracts from Raisa's thesis for the first time outside the Soviet Union. I decided that the best way to provide the Western reader with the essence of Raisa's research was to present summaries of individual chapters in her thesis.

The first chapter, 'The Development of New Material Life-styles' dealt with consumer patterns of collective farm families compared with statistics describing the budgets of peasant families before the 1917 Revolution. Raisa outlined the growth of a network of business undertakings, the provision of goods and services for the population, the development of a system of services and the supply of a wide range of goods in rural areas of Stavropol, and analysed the statistical foundation of her report. She reached the conclusion that communal enterprises catering for the every-day needs of farm workers were playing a growing role and had established themselves as a characteristic feature of a con-temporary collective farm village. She also remarked on the 'inconsistent nature of the development of forms of social organ-ization within the life of a collective farm worker'. She identified a number of reasons for this inconsistency, which created a situ-ation in which a significant number of villagers could not make use of public services on a regular basis. The reasons included the way in which settlements were geographically scattered and public services situated at considerable distances from them, with roads in poor repair and few means of public transportation. She also emphasized that service industries were short of trained manpower, and that the low degree of mechanization in the production processes ultimately accounted for the way in which price and quality bore so little relation to workers' efforts. She concluded that only by eliminating such restrictive factors could living conditions in rural areas begin to be improved to the level of those in towns.

Chapter Two of Raisa's thesis, 'The Growth of Intellectual and Cultural Aspirations in the Daily Life of Collective Farm Workers: In What Form and to What Degree These Can Be Satisfied', analysed the meaning and place of art and culture in peasants' lives. Her research in villages in the Stavropol region revealed an increase in intellectual and cultural aspirations among peasants.

As evidence of this she pointed to a rising graph of library borrowings, more visits to the theatre, cinema and concerts. As well as a growth in actual numbers she detected a difference in the quality of the demand, a desire for artistic activity of a higher standard. Raisa did not hide the great gap between these heightened aspirations on the part of the peasants and the likelihood of their being realized, nor did she deny that the level of cultural amenities in villages was, in general, low and inadequate.

In the third chapter,'Changes in the Nature of Personal Relationships Within the Everyday Life of the Family', Raisa examined the pattern of village marriage and social relationships within marriage. She noted that social barriers to the choice of marriage partners had disappeared almost entirely, and that there was now a tendency for town and country marriages to become more alike. But she also recognized objectively that a number of restraints to the development of family and marital relationships continued to exist. 'Looked at realistically,' Raisa wrote, 'the woman collective farm worker, who has to do her housework as well as carry out her duties on the farm, faces not only a handicap to intellectual fulfilment but also an obstacle to the achievement of economic equality.'

From her researches the author draws these conclusions: the quality of life in villages has changed since the Revolution, and social injustices have been remedied. Clothes, furniture and housing are of better quality. Work is the foundation of this prosperity. The trading network throughout the country has been expanded, and communal provisioning introduced. Culture has entered the village. Country people are better educated; illiteracy exists only among the elderly. Books, radio and television have reached the peasant. New relationships between people have been made possible. However, the village lags behind the town in the fulfilment of its material and cultural intellectual needs. The standards of public services, trade, communal facilities, educational establishments, medical care, accommodation and the arts are noticeably lower.

Many of the barriers to parity of development between country and town, as described by Raisa more than twenty years ago, remain in existence today, as I can confirm from my own observations. The Communist-imposed economic structure of the vast territory of the Soviet Union is not able to cope with problems of social inequality. Today, although the Soviet Union has natural resources comparable with those of the USA, Russia is far from self-sufficient in terms of food production. The Soviet Union has shortages in every area. Nor are intellectual and cultural amenities widely developed. In this context one can read Raisa Gorbachev's thesis – written in 1967, remember, as an action programme for the remainder of the twentieth century, to lead an underdeveloped Russia into the future.

During the four years she was working for her doctorate Raisa was certainly no 'armchair scholar'. As often as she could, she lectured on the findings of her researches to important officials in the party and the government, drawing their attention to undesirable developments, and endeavouring to drum up support for an increased focus on artistic and cultural activities in rural areas. She spent a growing amount of time on the collective farms where she had chosen to pitch her research. She not only assembled statistics, she took a practical hand in the organization of leisure activities. She was always ready with a suggestion directed towards the improvement of living conditions in the villages.

Even a brief study of Raisa's dissertation convinces me that in spite of the restrictive circumstances under which she had to work at the time, she was nevertheless able to produce a report that was impressively objective. Her thesis was, I was told, the first Soviet academic research project into social problems among collective farm workers. Her study dealt with the conditions that were prevalent at the time, and a number of expressions she uses date her report as belonging to the 1960s. Her dissertation remains, however, of interest today, not so much because of its wide-ranging factual material as for its honesty of analysis, and because it took a good deal of courage at the time to ask those particular questions.

Her dressmaker, S. Karetnikova, told me that Raisa herself sometimes recalls experiences she had while doing her interviews in rural villages. Mrs Karetnikova told me: 'Madame Gorbachev once mentioned a questionnaire she asked village wives to fill in, asking whether they used household bleach. One woman from a collective farm wrote in the answer space: "Yes, I tint my eyebrows." This is in itself a trivial anecdote, but it does illustrate the principle that things taken for granted in the town were largely unknown in the country.'

Throughout her candidature Raisa passed all the requisite exams with distinction. Both in the compulsory subjects – dialectical and historical materialism – and in the optional ones – history and English – she was awarded the highest mark, 'Very Good'. She was examined in 1967 at the Lenin Pedagogical Institute on her thesis, or, officially, her 'Dissertation for the Attainment of the Academic Title of Doctoral Candidate in Philosophic Science'. One of the assessors was Professor Sergei Timofeyevich Gurdyanov, currently Professor of Philosophy at Moscow State University, a man with whom the Gorbachevs are still on friendly terms.

In his report Professor Gurdyanov said that Raisa's work was a serious scientific contribution to the solution of theoretical and practical social problems in rural areas. Her thesis was, he said, not the result of abstract speculation but was based on extensive empirical investigation and analysis of difficulties characteristic of the living conditions of collective farm workers. All the other adjudicating members of the board voted in Raisa's favour, and she was awarded her doctorate with a unanimous vote of the faculty.

Mikhail Gorbachev was not the man to forego the chance to share such an important day with his wife. He accompanied her to the university, ordered a magnificent congratulatory bouquet to be sent to 'Dr Raisa', and the day ended on the usual Russian high note of a splendid banquet.

I came across several publications of Raisa's writings in the course of my researches. One was a version of her doctoral thesis for a general readership; it was published in Stavropol in 1969 under the title, 'Peasant Life on the Collective Farm: A Social Summary'. Publication in abridged form of a learned work is of course the usual way of widening the potential readership of specialist research.

In 1973 Raisa published a pamphlet in Stavropol entitled, 'The Twenty-Fourth Congress of the Soviet Communist Party and the Further Development of Socialist Culture', which signalled that her intellectual interest was moving from sociology towards culture in its widest sense. Her focus remained practical; she concentrated on particular projects she regarded as essential in education and the arts in the Stavropol region. She advocated building or refurbishing 233 schools, setting up at least forty boarding-schools, and opening of an arts centre in every village. She condemned the provision of libraries as 'wholly inadequate'. Her list of new projects for the villages was in tune with the aims that her husband had set himself to achieve as First Secretary of the Communist Party of the Stavropol Region.

In 1986 Raisa became a member of the governing body of the Soviet Cultural Foundation. It was a logical progression from her academic work and her activities within the community. 'You can see the hand of Raisa in the present rehabilitation of Russian culture.' says Professor Gennady Osipov, outlining her present role.

'Raisa Gorbachev is Vice-President of the Soviet Cultural Foundation, and few things occur now within the programme of cultural restoration in Soviet Russia without her having some say in them. Influence on social and cultural life can, I believe, be exerted not only through books and articles or even through making practical proposals, but by personal attitudes and example. Culture is a social phenomenon – perhaps, in my view, the most important element in sociology, which I define as the analysis of social behaviour. The profundity of a society's culture can be measured by the extent to which the social behaviour of its members is influenced by their cultural heritage. A man has the choice between acting in response to accepted social norms and values or adopting markedly antisocial attitudes. Within this concept of culture I find it entirely natural for Raisa Gorbachev to have moved directly from her preoccupation with the living conditions of peasants on collective farms to a commitment to culture.

'Raisa Gorbachev is only one of a host of men and women who have, through their open support of sociology, which was this country's first socially progressive movement, made a significant contribution to *glasnost* and *perestroika*. Given the conditions of the time her attitude was new, remarkable, brave, strong and impressive.'

I thought Professor Osipov would probably know whether Raisa Gorbachev, with her self-confidence and social commitment, had initiated a trend towards the involvement of women in Soviet society. When I asked him, he prefaced his reply by saying that in 1988 Raisa had promised to take part in a symposium at the Academy of Sciences on the subject of the participation of women in society. 'But something prevented her from attending, and we all regretted this very much,' he said.

'You must remember that the attitude of the Soviet general public to the wife of a top political leader is not the same as in the West. Raisa Gorbachev as a sociologist must be aware of this. If she were to make a well-publicized pronouncement on any subject, this would without doubt inspire an adverse reaction; it would be seen as an incursion into areas where she had no place. If, for instance, Raisa, as the wife of the head of the Kremlin, were to become active in a woman's movement, you can be sure that critics would say there were many other problems far more deserving of her attention. I personally cannot accept all our traditions, but you make a large mistake if you ignore them.

'It is possible to think of several reasons why Raisa is not too popular with some sections of the population. Firstly, you have a prejudice dating back to Stalin's time, the view that the wife of any government or party leader should remain apart from all social and political activity. Secondly, you have the age-old Russian tradition, which still runs deep in the public consciousness, that a wife is ordained to occupy a lower rung on the social ladder than her husband. Today the large Muslim minority in the Soviet Union reinforces this patriarchal attitude.'

Professor Osipov said that many Soviet women had *petit bourgeois* values, so that when they saw the wife of a Soviet leader playing a conspicuous role in public life they condemned her, even when her prominence had positive advantages for the Soviet Union.

'I know that in America, for instance,' he added, 'if a President's wife dresses carelessly, unfashionably or dowdily, she could cost her husband votes at the next election. In Soviet Russia, by contrast, if the wife of a high-ranking official appears in a variety of outfits, looking smart, she meets with severe disapproval, the more so because we have no tradition of elegant political wives. You only have to think of the wives of Khrushchev, Brezhnev or Andropov. People say: "How can that woman dress so well and look chic when in this country we don't have enough clothes to go round?" '

What of the reactions when a political wife like Raisa pursues a high-profile academic career? Professor Osipov said that this, too, brought criticism. Some people said she was simply trying to grab the limelight for herself. He himself saw these *petit bourgeois* reactions as rooted in envy, which meant that someone like Raisa Gorbachev was often exposed to spiteful hostility.

'Some of our traditions are primitive and barbaric,' he said, 'and I think it will take quite a time to adjust Russian modes of thinking and bring them into line with European culture. Will Raisa reap the benefits of such changes? Here I'm a bit of a pessimist. Regrettable as it may be, I believe, as so often, the Bible is right, and a prophet is not without honour save in his own country.'

5

Return to Moscow

The career of Mikhail Gorbachev himself was shaped by dramatic changes of circumstances, in which luck played its part. It is undoubtedly true that he rose to the top in Stavropol through his outstanding achievements. Under his leadership even the agricultural economy of the region, which had been a problem child everywhere else in the Soviet Union, showed an improvement in production. His predecessor in the post of First Secretary of the Communist Party of the Stavropol Region, F. D. Kulakov, was transferred to Moscow as Head of the Agricultural Department of the Central Committee, giving him an ideal position from which to act as advocate for his successor in Stavropol. But in 1978 Kulakov suddenly died. He was only sixty years old, and no member of the party leadership attended his funeral, which gave rise in Moscow to rumours of mysterious events, personal rifts, even of suicide. As well-known party leaders either could not through some circumstances attend, or decided personally not to go to Kulakov's funeral, the delivery of the oration was assigned to a party official almost unknown outside his own region, Mikhail Gorbachev.

Neither Gorbachev's achievements nor Kulakov's recommendation would in themselves have assured Gorbachev of a summons to Moscow. Gorbachev's route to the top was smoothed by an illness – yes, an illness – not one that affected him personally, but the kidney problems from which Yuri Vladimirovich Andropov, then the powerful head of the KGB, convalesced regularly in the Stavropol region, where he often met Gorbachev. Mikhail was a considerate host to party VIPs – Prime Minister Kosygin was also a frequent visitor to the spa – and with Raisa's intelligent help in these social duties he made a series of useful connections.

Raisa undoubtedly knew how to play her part and was unquestionably a surprise to the Moscow leadership. They had not expected to find someone with her personality as the wife of a regional official in a provincial city. Long walks with Madame Andropov, on which Raisa talked about her beloved Moscow, helped to strengthen the friendship between the Gorbachevs and the Andropovs. The Gorbachevs carefully held the delicate balance between familiarity and discretion, allowing their guests to enjoy their holiday undisturbed, but on hand when the guests required anything. It was, I think, a situation in which no husband and wife could work as partners better than the Gorbachevs.

The Andropovs were so taken by Raisa's feminine charm that the two couples spent a leave together in Kislovodsk in 1977. The Andropovs were under the care of a pleasant sanatorium called Red Stones, staying in a dacha that had been built for them in the heart of a nature reserve. The Gorbachevs were in a nearby sanatorium, Blue Stones, neither so expensive nor so grand. But the two couples could, if they so wished, meet or go for walks every day. They seem to have got along together very comfortably, and it may well be that the success of that joint holiday finally persuaded Andropov to think seriously of transferring Mikhail Gorbachev to Moscow. Andropov could not immediately settle the timing of this move. The transfer had to be effected at an opportune moment.

On 28 November 1978 *Pravda* announced that Comrade Mikhail Sergeyevich Gorbachev had been appointed a Secretary of the Central Committee. Neither the terms of reference for Gorbachev's post nor the circumstances of his selection were made public, but one can safely say that Raisa approved of her husband's promotion. She was always keen for him not to remain content with his successes, and her confident, self-assured personality was in itself a help to him. As her friend Lydia Budyka said: 'Raisa had decided that the most important thing in her life was to help her husband in every possible way. Their relationship is so close that Mikhail always likes to know that she is within call, so that they can talk and discuss things together. She is a friend as well as a wife.' Raisa had, and still has, a gift for knowing the best course of action in any situation. She can be opportunistic, while remaining straightforwardly determined, and she invariably calculates with great attention to detail. When one analyses the inner strengths that have taken Gorbachev to his present political eminence, one must not minimize the manner in which Mikhail and Raisa work in partnership.

When the Gorbachevs set off for Moscow again in 1978 they had not only more luggage, they had a bigger family. They had arrived in Stavropol some twenty years earlier with little more than two suitcases and some boxes of books. They now required a large removal lorry, not only for their own possessions but for those of their daughter Irina and son-in-law Anatoly, who were moving to Moscow as well. The Gorbachevs took over a five-room apartment with 200 square metres of living space in Alexei Tolstoy Street, in a party-owned residential block built specifically for members of the Central Committee.

Communist regimes, however, observe strict protocol in deciding which accommodation shall be alloted to whom. While the new apartment in Moscow was in some ways more luxurious than the last house the Gorbachev family had occupied in Stavropol, it was nowhere near as comfortably furnished as the townhouses of members of the Politburo. Towards the end of the 1970s the Soviet Union had begun to import some Western styles of domestic architecture. They no longer built utilitarian bedsitting apartments, but put more emphasis on aesthetics and comfort. The first to profit from this revised approach to architecture were, inevitably, the top officials in the party, and for some years domestic buildings designed along progressive Western lines were reserved exclusively for them and their families.

Raisa never regarded anywhere she lived as an interim solution, a temporary billet. Within a few days of moving into a new home she would give it the stamp of her individuality. She introduced flowers and potted plants, hung pictures on the walls, fixing all the small things that give a home a welcoming atmosphere. As in everything else she undertakes, she puts her heart and soul into her housekeeping; the word 'perhaps' does not seem to exist in her vocabulary. In this aspect of her personality Raisa differs from the majority of Soviet housewives, who are not especially concerned or imaginative about creating a home. It may be that her need to have a warm, welcoming home has its origins in her nomadic childhood, when for years on end her family lived in a railway goods wagon. She must have learnt from her mother then, how even the poorest accommodation can be transformed into a real home.

From the balcony of their spacious sitting-room in Alexei Tolstoy Street, the Gorbachevs could look out on one of Moscow's many parks, on old streets and alleyways and historic buildings. The leading Soviet interior designers had been employed to decorate their apartment, making extensive use of equipment and materials from the West. But the apartment block in which the Gorbachevs lived looked, from the outside, just like many other Moscow houses. This inconspicuousness is deliberate. Only a sentry-box in front of the entrance to the block indicates that it is not Ivan Ivanovich or any ordinary Soviet citizen who lives here.

To the right of the building stands the Dom Priyomov, a hall used for important receptions. Most of the other blocks in the neighbourhood belong to the KGB, the Soviet security force. The famous – or, if you like, notorious – 'No Name' restaurant, which criminals and dubious speculators (who, of course, exist in the Soviet Union as in any country) have made their headquarters, is situated close by. The clientèle of the restaurant are not small fry. Their names betray intimate links with the Communist Party apparat. Among the 'No Name' customers one finds Khrushchev's respectable grandson, a son-in-law of former Prime Minister Kosygin, and Brezhnev's daughter, who was known to have had a succession of affairs and whose corrupt deals frequently brought her into conflict with the law. It was only with the advent of *glasnost* and *perestroika* that these crimes became public knowledge.

The Gorbachevs lived in Alexei Tolstoy Street until the end of 1980, when Mikhail was made a full member of the Politburo, and had to move into an apartment reserved for this most élite of circles. I was determined to photograph the house in Alexei Tolstoy Street for my book about Raisa. I knew this would be a difficult project, but fortunately for me, a friend of mine knew someone who was friendly with the janitor of the apartment block opposite. A carton of Marlboro cigarettes did the rest.

I didn't enjoy going up with my camera in an old, rickety, badly-oiled lift, which shuddered and creaked until it finally landed me on the top floor. There was litter and building rubble everywhere; the wooden floor threatened to collapse at any minute. The wind whistled through the cracks. I wasn't keen to go any further. It crossed my mind that people would have been watching me from the KGB apartments. I hadn't noticed a beam and bumped straight into it. I couldn't find a good position for taking a picture, and I was about to give up, when suddenly a steel door opened and a stranger, who turned out to be the janitor, came and shook me by the hand. He led me out on to the flat roof. Standing there I could see the photograph I'd been aiming for. I had a view of the seventh floor, where the Gorbachevs lived when they first returned to Moscow. It was unoccupied, all the windows were closed. There were no curtains or blinds. Somebody told me later that this was by the Gorbachevs' express wish. They did not want their flat to be tenanted. I thought of the housing shortage in Moscow, of my Soviet friends living as a family of six or eight in two or three rooms, three generations together, with the grandchildren having no hope of a home of their own. None of my friends had the chance of a place like that. But the best accommodation in the Soviet Union is reserved for the highest-ranking officials. Nobody else can take it over.

I took my pictures and made my way carefully back to the lift. The street was quiet, the trees in full leaf. I looked again at the empty seventh floor where the Gorbachevs had lived. My friends were not specially interested. They had been standing in a queue for six hours to buy some meat and they were going to make *pilmeni*. That is a Russian dish I really like, small chunks of meat in a kind of dumpling dough. That is another small link with Raisa. *Pilmeni* are supposed to be her favourite dish.

At the end of 1980 the Gorbachevs moved into a new apartment in Shchusev Street, classified as 'Politburo category' and measuring 350 square metres. This time their block of flats belonged to the Brezhnev era, whose architectural style is marked by heavy concrete cladding, huge windows and imposing entrances. They lived in Shchuzev Street until 1985 when Mikhail Gorbachev was made General Secretary. Only the most privileged people in Moscow society lived there, among them Valentina Terechkova, the Soviet cosmonaut, and Brezhnev's daughter, Galina. While the cosmonaut has not moved, Brezhnev's daughter is now no longer a resident. When Gorbachev came to power, he ordered

97

a clean-up of the corrupt practices of his predecessors. It emerged publicly that Galina Brezhnev and her husband, Yuri Churbanov, who was a general and First Deputy of the Ministry of the Interior under Brezhnev, had used their positions of power to amass fabulous personal wealth, and were up to their necks in smuggling and corruption. It was also revealed that they had taken trunks full of valuables and irreplaceable works of art out of the country and had enriched themselves whenever possible at the Soviet people's expense. It was reported that 200,000 dollars in cash, and jewels worth about a million dollars, were found in their apartment. Churbanov was sentenced to ten years' imprisonment in 1988. His wife lost all her privileges, has become an alcoholic and lives in a psychiatric hospital.

Mikhail Gorbachev's appointment as General Secretary was officially announced on 11 March 1985. He was the eighth in line after Lenin. Andrei Gromyko, who had spent fifty years on the international circuit but had never been offered such a notable promotion, said in explanation that Gorbachev had a charming smile and exceptionally strong teeth. Which is a compliment that can now be paid to Raisa, who has indeed a charming smile and flawless teeth. In the Stavropol pictures they do not look so perfect; perhaps she had them capped in the 1980s.

With the move to Moscow, Raisa had given up her academic work. She would have had ample opportunity to lecture on sociology in Moscow, which is, of course the educational centre of the USSR. She put aside the professional opportunities open to her to devote herself completely to her husband's work. Though there is no official status for the wife of a Central Committee secretary or Politburo member, she made herself her husband's most effective aide. She assiduously pursued any new reports in the field of sociology, and when she thought them relevant, summarized them for his benefit. She provided her husband with continuous background material and up-to-date information on sociological topics. It can be said that she made a significant contribution to the formation of the ideas that Mikhail Gorbachev proclaimed to the world as *glasnost* and *perestroika* and incorporated in his political programme when he succeeded to the highest office in the Soviet Union.

6

Life in the Leadership

On the day that Mikhail Gorbachev became General Secretary, the lifestyle of his family was transformed abruptly into 'life at the top'. Leaders of the party and members of government are the beneficiaries of a system that has functioned for decades, and which was largely unchanged when Gorbachev came to power. Within this system an official's standard of living is strictly related to his rank. For instance, an actual member of the Politburo enjoys more privileges than a mere candidate for membership of the Politburo. Both members and candidate members of the Politburo are entitled to more than a Secretary of the Central Committee, and so on down the scale. In the highest echelons of the Soviet hierarchy material benefits include spacious living accommodation, which for all other Soviet citizens, even the well-off, is simply not available. They are provided with food of the finest quality and a wide range of free domestic help: chefs, waitresses, housemaids, chauffeurs. They have personal physicians. Soviet leaders can also look forward to free annual holidays at resorts on the Black Sea or the Baltic.

Politburo members are paid salaries of only 1200 roubles a month, while the monthly personal income of the owner of a successful co-operative restaurant might be 5000 to 8000 roubles. The average wage of a Soviet labourer is 234 roubles a month. Important scientists and leading writers and artists can all expect to earn more than top Soviet politicians. But the income of Soviet politicians and government functionaries is of secondary importance compared with the material advantages accruing from their official positions.

One crucial distinction between life in the Soviet Union and life in the capitalist West is the question of purchasing power. In West Germany 100 Deutschmarks are worth just as much in an ordinary worker's pocket as they are in a government minister's pocket; they can buy him just as much. But in Soviet Russia, Raisa Gorbachev's 100 roubles might as well belong to a different currency from the 100 roubles in the purse of an ordinary Soviet housewife. As the wife of a high-ranking politician, Raisa can use her roubles to buy any goods she chooses from any country she wishes. The Soviet housewife can only buy from the thinly stocked shelves of Soviet shops. I found this aspect of Soviet life difficult to comprehend, having been brought up from childhood to believe that you can buy what you want, providing you have the money.

The significance of the privilege factor in the Soviet Union as compared with the money factor is illustrated most obviously in living accommodation. Even the most prosperous Soviet citizen has no chance of acquiring one of the spacious flats or houses reserved for the leadership. He could not purchase a luxury flat for his entire personal fortune. He would be ruled out because he does not belong to the magic circle of privileged officialdom.

Since 1985 the Gorbachevs have lived in the accustomed style of Soviet leaders, spending most of their time out of town in a dacha. (I am not referring to a 'weekend cottage', as 'dacha' is often translated in the West, but to an imposing country estate.) Most of the high-ranking Soviets live in dachas situated within a thirty-kilometre radius of the Kremlin. The dachas of the highest officials in the party and the government lie west of Moscow, along Rublev Avenue.

Until recently no publicity was given to the life and lifestyle of the Soviet first family. But because of Gorbachev's policies of *glasnost* and *perestroika*, people in the Soviet Union became more openly critical. They wanted to know whether all the privileges were necessary and they wanted information about the lifestyle of the leadership. At the Congress of People's Deputies in March 1989, the criticism found expression. In reply, Mikhail Gorbachev described his living accommodation: 'We have a house in town. Neither I nor members of my family has a private dacha. In consideration of their duties, government dachas are put at the disposal of senior government members. The dacha allocated to the General Secretary of the Central Committee of the Communist Party and the President of the Supreme Soviet fulfils a particular function and is equipped accordingly. It can accommodate a meeting of the Politburo or of the Supreme Soviet, or a reception for heads of state from other countries. It has an office, a library and a communications centre with the most up-to-date equipment. There are also technical installations, which are essential to the executive function of the Chairman of the Soviet Defence Committee. Only a portion of the accommodation at the dacha is for the private use of the family.'

Rublev Avenue is not a wide boulevard, but its importance shows in the careful maintenance of its tree-lined length. It is hard to remember in this romantic setting that one is only a few kilometres from stifling, dirty, industrial Moscow. There is no rush of traffic. All lorries are forbidden access and only a few cars use the narrow, two-lane avenue. The bulk of passing traffic consists of government cars, black Volgas or Chaikas; occasionally a Zil limousine glides past, which means that one of the inner circle of Kremlin leaders is on the way to or returning from his dacha.

The use of Zil limousines is restricted to members of and candidates for the Politburo, and secretaries of the Central Committee. The windows of the Zils are of opaque security glass, so that observers cannot see who is in the limousine. If the passenger is Mikhail Gorbachev, the car will be at the centre of a convoy of high-speed security vehicles. The lead car will be the KGB Mercedes, next one or two black Volgas, then come two Zils together, and following the Zils a Zil station wagon, which is an ambulance, with a black Volga completing the column. Security precautions ensure that no observer knows in which of the two Zils the President is riding, on his own or accompanied by members of his family. Gorbachev and his family move everywhere with a permanent bodyguard numbering between seven and twelve, whose commander sits like a shadow with the President in the Zil; other members of the security squad ride in the two Volgas in the convoy, with more bodyguards in the second or decoy Zil. Doctors and nurses are present in the ambulance.

The security police have used Mercedes since the 1970s when

101

the then Soviet Minister of the Interior, Shcholokyov, authorized the purchase of a substantial number of West German cars, setting up the only service station in Moscow for this type of Mercedes. It is still open today. Sons of high-ranking Soviet officials sometimes drive a Mercedes. For instance, Gorbachev's son-in-law, Anatoly, has a grey 280S Mercedes automatic.

Raisa has a Chaika for her private use and is always accompanied by one or two security officers. These personal bodyguards are known by Russians as 'second shadows', for their security brief is to stick to their charges as closely as a shadow.

It is exceptional for a woman in the Soviet Union to have a driving licence; neither Raisa Gorbachev nor her daughter, Irina, possesses one. In any case neither Mikhail nor Raisa would be permitted by the security officers to take the wheel. The risk would be too great. There can be exceptions to security rules, as I can testify from personal observation. On Friday 14 July 1989 the Supreme Soviet was in session until late in the evening. At the close of the meeting Gorbachev invited his colleagues to dinner at his town house in Kosygin Street. The fleet of Zils belonging to the ministers waited until 11 pm, when all the Zils drove off in the direction of Rublev Avenue. On the Saturday at 10.30 am, a lone Zil with no escorting security cars arrived at the entrance of Gorbachev's residence in Kosygin Street, and Gorbachev himself, wearing a light summer suit, stepped out and disappeared into the house, leaving the chauffeur to park the car. Within a quarter of an hour Mikhail and his wife, Raisa, who had spent the night in the town house with her daughter Irina, came out into the street laughing, arm in arm. The Zil chauffeur in his shirtsleeves jumped out of the car to open the door, but Gorbachev intervened to help his wife, who was wearing a casual white linen suit, into the Zil himself and then climbed in beside her. I saw no security men anywhere around, so it does seem that the Soviet First Family can occasionally make a private sortie through Moscow.

The drive from the Kremlin, or the offices of the Central Committee of the Soviet Communist Party, or the headquarters of the Cultural Foundation, to the Gorbachevs' dacha takes no more than twenty-five minutes. You turn off Rublev Avenue and drive along a narrow asphalt road, within a few minutes you arrive at the fence enclosing the dacha. All Government dachas have similar security perimeter fences, almost three metres high, with a thin electrified wire running along the top. Behind massive double gates is a guardhouse manned twenty-four hours a day. The officer of the watch received me when I visited the dacha.

The officers and men who guard the President and his family are volunteers from the KGB. This bodyguard is divided into two groups. The first is the External Group, consisting of twelve guards who provide permanent escorts for Mikhail and Raisa Gorbachev on private and official journeys in Moscow, the rest of the Soviet Union and on foreign trips. The second or Internal Group is responsible for guarding the presidential dacha and townhouse round the clock; in security jargon, it 'protects the target'. The number of people on guard at the dacha at any one time is governed by the presence of the master of the house. When Gorbachev is not in residence, the security men near the main gate are reinforced by three or four guards patrolling the grounds. When Mikhail Gorbachev is staying at the dacha, guards are stationed at regular intervals along the fence. The drive to the house (from the fence to the dacha is a distance of three or four kilometres) is monitored by an electronic warning system. In the woods surrounding the dacha are almost invisible tripwires close to the ground. Should anyone try to approach the house, touching off a tripwire, the warning system sounds an alert, and a group of security men and guard dogs instantly surround the area.

A commandant, usually holding the KGB rank of colonel, is responsible for both the security of the dacha and the maintenance of the house and grounds. The guard itself consists of professional soldiers from the KGB 9th Corps, which looks after the security of families of members of the Politburo and Central Committee, candidates for membership of the Politburo and Central Committee secretaries. All the household staff, including chefs, maids and gardeners, hold a military rank, and are, generally, trained professional soldiers.

Once through the entrance gates, you drive slowly along a narrow approach to the house. The grounds of the Gorbachev dacha are large and covered almost entirely with mixed woodland, pine and spruce predominating, but with numerous bushes and shrubs. In front of the house and on the side overlooking the path to the river are flowerbeds, some planted in precise, symmetrical shapes. Raisa, who loves flowers and plants,

103

supervises the garden herself. On a state visit to Cuba, for instance, she continually demanded the names of plants and flowers from her interpreter, wanting to know which of these tropical blooms might be cultivable in Moscow. In the Gorbachevs' dacha garden are gladioli, asters and tulips. Raisa also manages to grow roses, which as a rule do not flourish in the Moscow climate, in considerable numbers. Lilac trees are planted round the house. Lilac is called 'the Russian rose' in Germany, because Russians grow it in such profusion. White and purple lilac blooms are at their most fragrant in May and June, producing a scent which Raisa loves. The dacha has a large greenhouse in its grounds, with a humid subtropical temperature, for growing both vegetables such as gherkins, tomatoes and pumpkins, and flowers, including orchids, roses, carnations, narcissi, crocuses and plants that Raisa Gorbachev has brought back from her trips overseas. Near the perimeter one finds a fruit garden with apple and pear trees, plum and cherry, even raspberries and redcurrants flourishing. Peacocks, pheasants and guinea-fowl wander through the garden. The peacocks and the pheasants, which come from the south of Russia, have evidently become acclimatized to the Moscow winter, for they survive the cold.

Gardeners and groundsmen maintain the garden, flowerbeds and greenhouse. Everything in the garden has to be carefully tended, the trunks of the fruit trees protectively painted white, the flower and vegetable beds tidily weeded. The woodlands, too, are kept in good order; diseased and dead trees felled, overgrown bushes cleared away, but systematically, to ensure that the woodlands' natural wildness is not spoilt. Nature lovers would notice that few people use the woods, which are alive with birdsong and provide a habitat for all kinds of small woodland creatures. It is in its way a pocket nature reserve, managed so that it suffers minimal disturbance by man. The woods extend almost to the main building, with little paths leading in all directions. Whichever path you take from the centre you are within half an hour's brisk walk of the broad path encompassing the grounds of the dacha. to walk this circular footpath, which runs alongside the perimeter fence, takes at least two hours.

When you return to the main building, you discover that it is linked to other buildings by covered walkways, one of which leads to a low, one-storey structure of glass and metal, containing a swimming pool and a sauna. In summer the wall of the swimming pool can be moved aside at the touch of a switch, enabling the swimmer to emerge alongside the woodlands and flower gardens. Placed round the pool are lightweight Finnish wicker chairs, rocking chairs and garden loungers with floral-patterned cushions. The colour of the water in the pool, which is tiled in bright blue, can be altered at will, from the dark blue of the sea in good weather to the pale green of a stormy sea near the shore. This 'sea change' probably reminds the Gorbachevs of their dacha at Pitsunda on the Black Sea coast. At dusk the pool is illuminated by searchlights.

To get from the swimming pool to the sauna you walk down a short flight of marble steps, entering a relatively large room, panelled throughout in light-coloured wood, and housing a huge stove, a large, sturdy wooden table, benches and stools, all imported from Finland. Soft, comfortable chairs are arranged in a semi-circle around the stove, and a massive, heavy, wooden-handled door leads to the Finish sauna itself, which provides dry steam heat. For some twenty years ownership of a Finnish sauna has been a status symbol in the Soviet Union. Senior and junior functionaries built saunas in their dachas and in town, until the point was reached when a family without a sauna of its own had no social status whatsoever.

Another passageway from a wing on the other side of the house leads to utility rooms, kitchen, larder and domestic servants' sitting room. The kitchen is large and furnished with up-to-date equipment, all imported from the West: a big cooker, worktables and many different electrical appliances. The domestic servants' rooms are comfortably, plainly furnished, reminding you of an ordinary Soviet hotel room. A television set stands in a small vestibule, beyond which is the servants' dining-room.

The government dacha is a large, two-storey building of nearly 1000 square metres in size. Most of the official dachas date from the period between the 1930s and the beginning of the 1950s which is approximately the Stalinist era. They are relatively uniform in architectural style, building materials and interior decoration. They are generally rectangular with a handsome rear verandah. They are built of brick rendered with yellow stucco and have dark green metal roofs with a flat area for sunbathing or sport in summer. The architecture belongs largely to the constructivist style, or the modernism of the 1930s and 1940s. They remind you of Le Corbusier. The Soviet architects who designed and built these houses owed much to the important Swiss architect, who himself worked in the Soviet Union several times. The Hotel Moskva in the centre of Moscow, not far from Red Square, is one of the buildings constructed to his design. Stalin liked Le Corbusier's style and recommended it to Soviet architects.

The cost of building the government dacha occupied by President Gorbachev and his family in Rasory, as the dacha complex off Rublev Avenue is called, was around six million roubles, which excludes fixtures and fittings, but includes the cost of a helipad, a news communications centre and a house with apartments for official guests. The central building has some twenty rooms, the largest of which are the dining-room, private cinema and billiard room. All the furniture was made at the Lux factory in Moscow, as it would have been in Stalin's time. The décor also belongs to the Stalinist period: wood panelling, massive leather furniture and heavy curtains. One feature common to all official dachas are the 'Kremlin runners' in the corridors, narrow strips of raspberry-red carpet with green borders and fine edging of sand-coloured stripes. Dacha floors are of dark brown oak parquet, but guest rooms have two-tone parquet flooring.

Inside the dacha there are flowers and decorative house plants everywhere, in pots and bowls. In the conservatory, which is kept at a subtropical temperature, can be found a range of plants and trees, many rare in Russia. When the world outside is in the grip of snow and ice, indoor palm and orange trees look startlingly exotic.

In general, the Gorbachev dacha is comfortable and luxurious, and yet the atmosphere is a little cool. You don't have the feeling that one family has lived here for generations, which is only natural, since it is, for the present occupants as well, an official residence.

The presidential dacha has a staff to match its many demands, and the employees fall broadly into four categories: gardeners, groundsmen; maintenance staff such as electronic engineers, electricians, plumbers, carpenters; kitchen and serving staff; and general domestics. Both men and women are employed as chefs in government dachas, but the head chef is usually male. Domestics work under the command of a woman housekeeper, who organizes the housework and supervises the kitchen, and is in her turn answerable to the dacha's chief steward. Recruits for employment in the President's dacha face a comprehensive vetting procedure, in which their general health and personal integrity are screened. Before they can be appointed they must sign a declaration that they will reveal no details about the dacha and its occupants during or after their period of service. Everything must remain top secret.

Meissen porcelain, both figurines and vases, is prominently displayed in the sitting-rooms. The collection is Raisa's pride, and only domestic staff authorized by her are allowed to dust these treasures. Some of the porcelain was given to her on trips to East Germany, the home of the Meissen factory. Once on a state visit to Cuba Raisa spotted a vase in a museum in the Old Town of Havana, lifted the valuable object from its plinth, to the consternation of the curator, saying delightedly: 'Ah, Meissen!' and launched into a résumé of what she had learnt during a tour of the Meissen factory. There are individual pieces in Raisa's collection which were made in pre-revolutionary days. The oldest comes from the Gardner factory, which belonged to a German–Dutch company based in St Petersburg, where the famous Kuznetzov porcelain was produced for the Romanov tsars. And, like the tsars, Raisa has a taste for Fabergé *objets d'art*.

Provisions for the Gorbachev family are supplied by the state. When Mikhail Sergeyevich Gorbachev became General Secretary, his family stopped buying food and groceries in special nomenklatura shops. Everything is ordered and delivered directly to the house or dacha. Raisa personally plans the family meals on a weekly basis, but she has to take her proposed menus to the presidential dietician for vetting. By order of the Politburo he has the right to make the final decision on what may or may not be cooked.

Both in the townhouse and the dacha, the kitchen is under the control of the KGB, and all food for the President is taken from the kitchen in small containers to KGB officers for official tasting. The food tasters are known in Russia as 'mushroom men', since they would be the first victims of any mysterious – say, mushroom – poisoning. I understand that no fewer than ten people have to testify with signatures and rubber stamps that the food is safe. Raisa Gorbachev is herself banned from cooking, and while she accepts many of the restraints arising from her position as President's wife without demur, she finds this prohibition hard to bear. She loves cooking, and used to collect recipes from university colleagues in Stavropol. Now she cannot cook for her husband, because the ever-suspicious world of security sees it as theoretically possible that she could poison him.

Food security is meticulously observed wherever the President may be, at home or abroad. It was even followed when Mikhail visited his mother, in his home village of Privolnoye. His mother, to whom he is devoted, and calls 'Baba Manya' (Grandma Manya), is forbidden to cook anything for the President. She pleaded in vain with the KGB when he visited her in the summer of 1988: 'Please let me prepare a meal for my son!' The KGB said no, continuing their unvarying routine in which the same officers who taste the food samples take the food containers back to the kitchen and supervise everything until the moment the President is served.

The family larder is kept stocked from various sources. As the lady of the house, Raisa puts in her daily order through the housekeeper to a food warehouse in Tranovski Street or to the food department of GUM, the store familiar to all Moscow visitors. Perishable food is of course dealt with quickly, while products that have a longer shelf life are delivered once or twice a month.

While collecting details about the Gorbachevs' diet I heard an anecdote, which strikes me as revealing, not least of the new public attitudes created by *glasnost* and *perestroika*.

Two friends meet in a Moscow street. One asks the other: 'Have you seen the latest photo of Raisa Gorbachev?'

'No, why?'

'It shows her weeping bitter tears.'

'That's not possible.'

'Oh yes it is, she'd lost her sugar coupons.'

In May 1989 sugar rationing was introduced, and every citizen was issued with coupons. Each coupon allowed you to buy 2 kilos of sugar at about 94 kopecks or roughly one pound sterling a kilo. The reason for this rationing was connected with Mikhail Gorbachev's anti-alcohol campaign. To improve public health and reduce drunkenness, he promulgated laws severely restricting the sale of alcohol. Some drinkers set up illicit stills, and the demand for sugar (which is used to make 'bootleg liquor') soared.

The general public, as this anecdote illustrates, has become more openly critical of the privileged treatment of officials in the distribution of food. People would say that as long as the wives of high-ranking members of the government and party didn't have to shop themselves, or queue at the collective farm market, conditions wouldn't improve for ordinary citizens. At the centre of the criticism were the 'health-food stores', distribution centres for rationed goods for officials only. One can be found in the heart of Moscow, near the Kremlin. From midday on, the narrow thoroughfare of Tranovski Street was usually choked with Volgas and Chaikas, belonging to the wives of senior officials collecting the family 'food ration'. Under Gorbachev the system has been almost entirely abolished; special food distribution exists only for the members and candidates for the Politburo and Secretaries of the Central Committee. In the grey everyday life of the Soviet Union some types of food are simply unobtainable, and the number of the privileged may well have been reduced out of necessity as much as principle.

From the early years of the USSR, the ruling class has received privileged medical treatment in exclusive hospitals, controlled by an administrative section listed until the end of the 1930s as the Health Medical Department of the Kremlin. Every family in the privileged class had its own physician, usually a professor, who would look after the general health of the family, calling in a consultant when the need arose. The family physician made house calls, and when it was necessary for patients to go to hospital, they were taken to the Kremlin Hospital on the corner of Tranovski Street and Kalinin Prospect, only 500 metres from the walls of the Kremlin.

You can still see the grey, three-storey hospital building today. The names of the wards commemorate Stalin, Khrushchev, Brezhnev ... (It was here that some victims of police brutality during interrogation, such as beatings with rubber truncheons and electric shock tortures, were taken for medical treatment.) The interior of the 'Kremlyovka' has hardly changed since the mid-1930s: corridor walls and waiting-rooms panelled in oak, floors covered with 'Kremlin runners', heavy leather furniture in the consulting-rooms. The doors are so massive they look as if they

109

belonged to a gloomy medieval castle. It remains the most secret of hospitals – hence its use for victims of torture in the past – and today only the highest-ranking officials are treated there. Departmental ministers and more junior members of government are admitted to the First Polyclinic, a hospital situated in a quiet turning off Arbat Square in the centre of Moscow. There are, of course, other specialist clinics for the nomenklatura class, including one in a southwest Moscow district that one might regard as fashionable, as it has no factories in it.

One main health centre for Soviet VIPs is located away from downtown Moscow in Kopsevo on Rublev Avenue, convenient for the government dacha complex. The centre consists of a series of clinics with facilities for the treatment of thousands of patients at the same time. The scope of the centre cannot be fully recognized by an observer, for it is situated in the middle of a forest, with its grounds enclosed by a thick security fence under permanent guard. It has a number of small separate units referred to as 'boxes'. In one of these 'boxes' Yuri Andropov, Gorbachev's mentor and one of his predecessors as General Secretary, spent the last months of his life from November 1982 to February 1984, with his wife at his side. Andropov suffered from a serious kidney complaint and needed constant dialysis. The 'boxes' are reserved for VIPs and are kept empty when not required for high-ranking government officials.

For the first time since Stalin took power the Soviet Union has a leader who is in healthy middle age. The Gorbachev family health care consists mainly in the regular monitoring of their well-being and in preventive medicine. They have on their medical staff a dietician, a physiotherapist and a masseur, and of course they have regular check-ups with their family physician. Mikhail and Raisa keep fit through daily calisthenics and massage, and they continue their health routine during their summer holidays in their dacha in Pitsunda. Although Mikhail Gorbachev and his family are basically fit and enjoy good health, there is always a small team of doctors close at hand, ready to provide medical assistance in an emergency. The head of state has, as one would expect, the services of the most eminent specialists in the country at his disposal. Most of the leading doctors in the Soviet Union are registered as medical consultants with the 4th Department of the Ministry of Health, which is responsible for the medical welfare of the leadership and the highest grades of government officials. Academician E. I. Chazov was for many years head of this department – 'our specialist and friend', as Leonid Brezhnev called him at a medal-giving ceremony in the Kremlin. Chazov was Minister of Health under Gorbachev, but his connections with the Soviet leadership were severed. Brezhnev and many former officials of the Soviet leadership have been discredited, but some of their confidants remained in positions of trust. To cite another immediate example: A. T. Medvedyev, who was formerly Brezhnev's bodyguard, is now Gorbachev's head of security. This may represent an anomaly in the Soviet administrative structure, or possibly the survival power of able civil servants.

Professor Chazov was never the physician directly concerned with the health of the Gorbachev family, but for a period he did have overall responsibility for any medical treatment that Mikhail and Raisa underwent. Chazov has an international reputation in the medical field. He is deputy chairman of the movement 'Doctors for Peace', which campaigns internationally against nuclear and chemical weapons, and it was he who proposed that Gorbachev should seek the advice of a leading US authority on radiation effects, Dr Robert Gale, who went to Chernobyl after the disaster. The family doctor to the Gorbachevs is Vladimir Yarigin, director of No. 2 Medical Institute in Moscow, where their daughter Irina is a lecturer.

One must go back to 1966 to find evidence of a serious illness in Raisa Gorbachev. She had been aware of abdominal pain, but she was so busy with academic work that she did not complain, kept warm and did not go to the doctor. She was dancing with Mikhail at an official reception when she suddenly went deathly white. He drove her at once to the regional hospital in Stavropol, where Professor Yuri Gibezki diagnosed a burst appendix and operated successfully that same night. I cannot help feeling that her prompt and efficient treatment owed something to the fact that she belonged to the nomenklatura.

Irina wears contact lenses for myopia. Her mother has recently taken to wearing spectacles for reading on the advice of a distinguished Soviet eye surgeon, Dr Svyatoslav Fyedorov, who incidentally operated successfully on Gorbachev's cousin, Fedya Rodchenko, the present director of administration for the

111

Privolnoye district, where Gorbachev was born.

Major institutions in the Soviet Union such as the Academy of Sciences, the Writers' Union and individual government ministries have their own clinics, just like the party leadership. The standard of care and treatment is, generally speaking, much higher than in the polyclinics and hospitals where the Soviet man in the street must go for treatment. Medical care is indeed free for everybody in the Soviet Union; the state provides the necessary means. Under the constitution, all Soviet citizens have an equal right to the state's provision of health services. The reality is that from ten to fourteen times as much is spent on treating a patient in Moscow's No. 4 hospital for high-ranking officials, as on a patient in the public hospital only a few yards away. This differing treatment has been a target for public criticism, but so far, in contrast to the radical changes in the food supply system, the imbalance in health care between officials and the general public remains unaltered. Health is one of the most valuable human possessions, which probably explains why officials find these privileges the hardest to surrender.

As well as the dacha in Rublev Avenue the Gorbachevs have a townhouse in Moscow. When time is short, they cannot always get back to the dacha in the evening.

When the Soviet government was transferred from Petrograd in 1918 and Moscow became the capital of the USSR, Lenin and his closest colleagues moved into quarters in the Kremlin itself – not the magnificent rooms that had been occupied by the tsars, but the modest accommodation once used by the tsar's entourage and retinue of servants. No General Secretary of the Soviet Communist Party has ever occupied the tsarist suites since the Revolution of 1917. In the 1920s and 1930s Stalin and contemporary members of the Politburo continued to live in service quarters within the Kremlin walls, furnished in a uniform style with solid wooden furniture, and leather armchairs with canvas covers in summer. They also had the use of a splendid six-storey mansion in Tranovski Street. Before the Revolution the mansion had been home to members of the bourgeoisie: poets, novelists, actors. The new élite dismantled its elegance, consigning fine furniture and paintings to government warehouses and furnishing the apartments in dreary Kremlin style. Some of the rooms stood empty most of the time. They provided overnight accommodation for members of the Central Committee who were not stationed in Moscow, and who only came to the capital for committee meetings or on Stalin's express orders. The head of the Red Army and the most important ministers also lived here. The outer wall of the mansion is studded with memorial plaques bearing the names of well-known Soviet families who occupied its rooms.

The death of Stalin in 1953 was seemingly a signal for some Soviet leaders to move out of the shadow of the Kremlin into newly built, comfortable one-family houses in southwest Moscow on the banks of the Moscow river, in a district known as Sparrow Hills, then Lenin Hills. The houses are separated from the street and also from neighbouring houses by high stone walls. Their architecture and design are reminiscent of the dachas, and their honey-coloured walls and dark green roofs have made them a familiar landmark for Muscovites.

The downfall of Khrushchev and the rise of Leonid Brezhnev brought another change in housing policy for the Soviet leadership. Brezhnev decided it was 'undemocratic' to live in such big houses; more 'democratic' housing was provided in quiet streets in central Moscow, ten to fifteen rooms with living space varying from 300 to 600 square metres. The Gorbachevs moved into an apartment like this in 1980.

The houses in the Lenin Hills are still maintained, but no one lives there permanently. They are sometimes used for the accommodation of important overseas visitors. Nearby stands the Hall of Receptions, containing facilities not available in the Kremlin: a private sports complex with rooms for physiotherapy, two tennis courts and an indoor swimming pool.

When Kosygin was Prime Minister in the mid-1970s, he moved into a new grey three-storey house, surrounded by low iron railings, in the Lenin Hills not far from the one-family houses. He occupied one floor which had modern communications equipment, a sauna, a small swimming pool and a conservatory for exotic plants within its 500 square metres of living space. He used to relax in his own roof garden. Two of his senior officials lived in separate apartments in the three-storey house.

Leonid Brezhnev always refused to have a house like Kosygin's built for him, choosing instead a spacious apartment in Kutuzovski Prospect, the broad avenue used by Politburo members on their journeys between office and dacha. He occupied a whole floor, specially refurbished for him. Later, at the end of the 1970s, new accommodation was arranged for him in the centre of Moscow, but for some reason he didn't like it and never moved in. In fact he seldom used the flat in Kutuzovski Prospect, preferring to live in the dacha full-time.

At the end of 1986 General Secretary Mikhail Gorbachev and his wife moved into a new townhouse in Kosygin Street in the Lenin Hills, where Kosygin's daughter and son-in-law are among their neighbours. It is a three-storey building of concrete rendered with yellow plaster, surrounded by a narrow, well-kept lawn and dark iron railings, and with a little flowerbed in front. Compared with the main thoroughfares in Moscow like Kalinin Prospect, Kosygin Street is quiet and peaceful, with tall old trees on the central reservation. From the back of the houses you have a superb view of Moscow. The Lenin Hills, as the Gorbachevs would know from their student days, are among the most beautiful places in Moscow. Before the Revolution Muscovites traced bridle-paths there and made carriageways for horse-drawn vehicles; they made excursions to the hills and the first ever cycle tracks in Russia were laid out there. Even today, especially in summer, city-dwellers love to relax in the green countryside at the foot of the Lenin Hills, which stretches for several miles along the banks of the Moscow river.

The ground floor of the Gorbachev town residence is given over to security squads, communications offices, the kitchen and a sitting-room for chauffeurs. On the first floor are rooms for medical treatment, including a massage room, plus a sauna and a swimming pool. The second floor holds two flats occupied by other senior members of the Soviet government, and Mikhail Gorbachev and his wife Raisa have the third floor as their private quarters, sharing these with their daughter Irina, her husband Anatoly and their children Xenia and Anastasia. Total living space for the two families measures some 500 square metres. At the back of the house is a helipad, and the house is equipped to receive global satellite programmes, enabling the Gorbachevs to watch television from the Western world as well as programmes from the eastern bloc.

While I was actually photographing the Gorbachev house something happened which confirmed for me that the age of *glasnost* and *perestroika* has really dawned. A Russian friend of mine had parked his Lada car near the house, and as we walked towards it, I took my pocket camera out of its case, found a good photographic position and took several pictures. I was describing my impressions when I realized my friend had vanished. He had seen before I did that a security guard, armed with a machine gun was heading towards me. The guard saluted. I held out my hand and explained to him why I wanted a good photograph of the house.

'Please take as many pictures as you require,' the security guard said. 'Can I help you? Mikhail Sergeyevich is across in the Kremlin at the moment, and Raisa Maximovna is at the dacha. Their daughter came back to the house only an hour ago to prepare for the reception that is to be given here tomorrow evening. Unfortunately at this moment I can't invite you into the grounds to take your pictures, but as we advance with *glasnost* and *perestroika* it may be different in a year's time. Until then . . . '

I could hardly believe my ears. Not so long ago my camera would have been ripped out of my hand, and I might well have been questioned by members of the KGB. And I should have had to reply . . .

7

Cultural Circles

Nothing is as it was. There has been a slaughter of sacred cows.
The appointment of Mikhail Sergeyevich Gorbachev as
General Secretary in 1985 is now universally regarded as a water-
shed in the history of the Soviet Union. Old and obsolete ideas
have been jettisoned and circumstances previously unthinkable
in the USSR have become the most natural things in the world.

When, for example, in the life of Soviet Russia, did the wife of
the General Secretary appear in the list of paid officials of the
Presidium of the Supreme Soviet, as a colleague of her husband,
with responsibility for matters of protocol and social questions,
including the field of women at work? The salary amounted to
several hundred roubles a month, and a government car went
with the job – not a state limousine, but a middle-range staff car,
a Volga, in addition to the Chaika provided for her personal use
as wife of the General Secretary. Things did not end there. On
13 November 1986 Raisa was chosen for another well-paid post.
She was appointed Vice-President of the Soviet Cultural Foundation, a government organization established in the new age of
perestroika, with the aim of conserving and promoting Soviet art
and culture. The Foundation's underlying belief is that only an
educated, cultured population can hope to solve the Soviet
Union's social and economic problems.

Raisa's monthly salary as Vice-President was 700 roubles.
When this became publicly known it created the first, if small,
scandal of the Gorbachev era. The General Secretary's wife paid
for her work? As if that family didn't have enough privileges

already! Professor Dmitri Likhachev from Leningrad receives no payment at all for his duties as President of the Foundation.

When the Cultural Foundation was set up, it was stated plainly that the position of president was an honorary one, carrying no payment, while the vice-president should be salaried. As a result of the public criticism of Raisa Gorbachev, the Foundation's constitution was modified to put her work for the organization also on an honorary basis. The controversy did not however damage the highly fruitful partnership between Professor Likhachev, internationally known as an expert on Russian art and history, and Moscow's First Lady. The bond between them reached back to the years when her railway-worker father, Maxim Titorenko, was sent to a labour camp for his open criticism of Stalin's agricultural policies. Maxim Titorenko was imprisoned in the infamous Solovetski labour camp, where he had the bunk next to Likhachev. When Maxim Titorenko was freed at the beginning of the Great Patriotic War to resume his work on the railways, he told his daughter Raisa about his conversations with Likhachev. The scholar had convinced him that the great tragedy of the Russian people was the theft of their true history and culture. The prison camp memories of her father, a straightforward, unsophisticated man, made a lasting impression on Raisa. They strengthened her belief that the countries of the Soviet Union had the right to their own ethnic culture, and that history should be presented in a true, not a propagandist version. Her creed remains: 'The Russian soul needs freedom.'

The government building housing the Cultural Foundation was formerly an office where the Soviet Ministry of Defence entertained overseas visitors. For some time this powerful ministry resisted the suggestion that it should hand over the building to a cultural organization. Until 1917 the building was owned by the Tretyakov family, whose name is preserved in that of the Tretyakov Gallery, home of a famous collection of Russian paintings and sculpture. The first floor has two large reception rooms, one of which, the Oak Room, is used for board meetings of the Foundation and for entertaining distinguished guests. Raisa supervises the upkeep of the building and the living and working conditions of the Cultural Foundation with meticulous care, ensuring regular supplies of instant coffee, Indian tea, caviare and other goods not readily available to ordinary Soviet citizens.

The working committee meetings of the Foundation take place regularly. One outspoken debate concerned the question of payment to valued colleagues. Raisa put forward her point of view as a matter of strict principle, advocating a reduction both in the scale of the fee and the number of recipients. Not surprisingly, her suggestion was unpopular, especially as her own lifestyle was so materially secure. Some of the counter-arguments insinuated that she was reminding people of her own honorary status in the Foundation. 'The time has not yet come,' she said, justifying the austerity of her proposal, 'when we can freely pay such high fees. We must work harder and do more for our country.'

Only two people working at the Cultural Foundation have long-standing relationships with Raisa: Professor Likhachev and Georgy Vassilievich Myasnikov, who is the executive chairman of the Foundation and responsible for its administration. Meetings of the presidium can last four or five hours from 10 to 11 am to 3 or 4 pm with only two short breaks for refreshments. As Vice-President, Raisa Gorbachev has no room reserved exclusively for her; she usually spends breaks in the executive chairman's office. On days when the governing committee meets formally, Myasnikov receives Raisa at the foot of the stairs and escorts her to the Oak Room. Raisa also works closely with Ivetta Nikolayevna Voronova, head of the fund-raising section of the Foundation, who arranges charity performances, concerts and exhibitions in which Soviet artists and actors take part for the financial benefit of the Foundation. Their heavy official diary seldom allows the Gorbachevs to attend these events.

I understand that almost all overseas delegations who visit Russia as guests of the Cultural Foundation express a wish to meet Raisa Gorbachev. It is a wish that is granted only in exceptional circumstances. One such event occurred on 9 October 1987, when as Vice-President she received a painting as a gift from Baron Heinrich Thyssen-Bornemisza, the art patron and collector. The painting was by Alessandro Magnasco, an Italian master of the late seventeenth and early eighteenth centuries, whose work is known in the Soviet Union and can be found in galleries in Moscow and Leningrad. 'Landscape with Figure' is considered to be one of his finest works, and Raisa was most happy to receive it on behalf of the Cultural Foundation. The painting hangs today in one of Russia's most famous galleries, the

Pushkin Fine Art Museum in Moscow. She thanked the Baron warmly for his goodwill gesture to the Soviet Union, saying how much it would be appreciated by the Russian people. 'The exchange of works of art brings mutual enrichment', she said, 'and promotes international understanding.'

Armand Hammer, the American millionaire and patron of the arts who has had close ties with the Soviet Union since the days of Lenin, was accorded a special honour. On 16 June 1988, at a board meeting of the Cultural Foundation, he was elected an honorary member. Dr Hammer, now in his nineties, has for decades had business dealings with the USSR, and in the years of extreme hardship he acquired paintings in exchange for grain shipments from the USA. Dr Hammer has a luxury apartment in Moscow not far from the Tretyakov Gallery, a flat which some cynics say is reminiscent of the Gallery itself, in that it is full of paintings from the Tretyakov which he obtained many years ago on favourable terms. Hammer is the only 'capitalist' from the West who has permission to fly in one of his two private aircraft (OX Y 1 and OX Y 2) in Soviet airspace without a Russian co-pilot as navigator.

On her trips abroad with her husband, Raisa takes her duties for the Cultural Foundation seriously. Every gift she receives at home or abroad that has any connection with art, she donates to the Foundation. On her return flight from a state visit to Great Britain in April 1989, Raisa Gorbachev had with her a reminder of Russian history, a portrait of Tsar Peter III. When Lord Gowrie, the former Minister of the Arts, presented her with the picture, he said 'It is a painting by your Russian artist Alexander Rokotov.' Raisa politely informed Lord Gowrie that Rokotov did not paint that himself. 'It is "school of Rokotov",' she said, as she thanked him. Tact and diplomacy have to be learnt. The picture hangs today in the Russian Museum in Leningrad.

The presents that Raisa Gorbachev takes with her on these state visits are chosen by her in her capacity as representative of the Soviet Cultural Foundation. During her state visit to West Germany, she handed to the Director of the Beethoven Museum a gift from the Cultural Foundation: 'As a memento of my visit to the Beethoven Museum I should like to present this manuscript music book, one of the most valuable documents from our Central Museum of Musical Culture in Moscow. Until now you had four

Right In 1984 Mikhail Gorbachev, accompanied by Raisa, returned to Stavropol on an official visit, during which they inspected the covered market. Even then Raisa understood how to draw Mikhail's attention to something, more or less discreetly.

Below Raisa in East Berlin in October 1989 with Sandra, her youngest fan. Raisa's bodyguard is in attendance.

The Gorbachevs occupy two floors of this house in Kosygin Street in the Lenin Hills in Moscow.

Two people who love nature. Mikhail and Raisa take a walk in the grounds of their dacha not far from Moscow.

Raisa on a trip to Berlin and Dresden, 1986. She visits the famous Old Masters gallery in Dresden.

During the hard times, books were often Raisa's only comfort. Reading and browsing among the shelves remain among her favourite pastimes.

Raisa has inspired in Mikhail her own love of the theatre. After the performance they are willingly photographed with the cast.

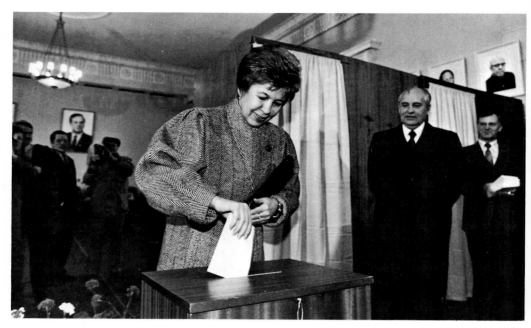

The election of People's Deputies in March 1989. Mikhail Gorbachev
watches his wife with interest.

1987: the first unofficial contact between the Russian Orthodox Church
and the Kremlin, prompted by the forthcoming millennium of the Russian
Orthodox Church in 1988. Patriarch Pimen (now deceased), with Mikhail
and Raisa.

Mikhail Gorbachev and his wife enjoy meeting the people. Here they talk to workers at a collective farm in Uzbekistan.

Mikhail and Raisa visiting the central reactor of the nuclear installation at Chernobyl, on 22 February 1989. Again the General Secretary talks to the workers, and his wife is an attentive listener.

Above The famous Russian fashion designer, Slava Zaitsev.

Left A sketch by Zaitsev, dedicated to Raisa. 'That is how I would dress Raisa Gorbachev,' he declares.

Right Tamara Makeyeva, Raisa's favourite Russian designer.

Below December 1986: Raisa attends the showing of Yves Saint Laurent's collection. Raisa's personal secretary, Gusenkev, is on the right.

The Queen receives the Gorbachevs at Buckingham Palace on their second visit to London.

Rapprochement between the Kremlin and the Vatican, November 1989. Mikhail Gorbachev, then General Secretary of the Communist Party of the Soviet Union, Pope John Paul II and Raisa.

December 1987: at a summit meeting in Washington, Nancy Reagan and Raisa Gorbachev meet at the White House. Two women who don't like each other.

December 1989: the Malta summit. Raisa talks to President Bush. Their respect for each other soon seemed to develop into a mutual trust.

Right Raisa's younger sister Ludmilla and her husband outside their house in Ufa. The resemblance to Raisa is striking.

Below Writer Yevgeny Titorenko with his favourite sister, Raisa, and Mikhail.

Right Raisa, Mikhail and his younger brother Sasha pay a short visit to Mikhail's mother, Maria, in 1983.

Below The Gorbachev clan at Mikhail's government dacha not far from Moscow. Front row, from left: Mikhail with his wife Raisa, his granddaughter Xenia and his mother Maria. Back row, from right, Maria's second son, Sasha Gorbachev; Irina, the Gorbachevs' daughter, and her husband, Anatoly Verganski; Luda, the daughter of Sasha and his wife, Sverta; Sverta, Raisa's sister-in-law.

Looking back on twenty-five years of marriage – Mikhail and Raisa in 1978.

Raisa opens her arms wide in greeting, a symbol of the glasnost that makes her so popular around the world.

pages from it, we have added 174 more,' she said.

The Soviet Cultural Foundation has for some time been creating reliable and important cultural connections with Western countries. Professor Ivan Timofeyevich Frolov, one of Mikhail Gorbachev's advisers on information and culture and editor-in-chief of *Pravda*, is closely concerned with the establishment of these links. Frolov has a significant influence on the President's philosophical and ideological thinking, and through him Raisa regularly receives catalogues of major art auctions in the West. Frolov also keeps her up-to-date with news of large exhibitions and cultural trends abroad. Most of his contacts are with academics specializing in Russian studies. These cultural links operate with a considerable degree of discretion and confidentiality, for some of the contacts may be asked to bid incognito at art auctions in the West on behalf of the Soviet Union. That was how, for instance, the letters of the great Russian writer Turgenev were bought at a 1989 auction in Baden-Baden for a five-figure sum, and passed into the possession of the Soviet Union. At Sotheby's in London, an unpublished letter by Pushkin was bought for the Cultural Foundation for £32,000, and £400,000 was paid for the manuscript of Turgenev's *Fathers and Sons*.

It is evident that the funds that Raisa controls are considerable. Her main job at the Foundation lies not in fund-raising, arranging benefits and charity concerts or readings from the great Russian poets. Instead, she is closely involved with the international art world. She is at the centre of negotiations with foreign countries and directs Russian strategic plans for the conservation of the arts. Her work for the Cultural Foundation is, in a sense, her secret weapon. It has given her the self-confidence to stand beside her husband in public in her own right, eschewing the passive role that wives of previous Soviet leaders have always played. As active Vice-President of the Foundation, she moves within the world of art on the international stage. She has her own place in her husband's arena.

Raisa's activities with the Cultural Foundation impinge on the Gorbachevs' private life. She is Mikhail's most important adviser on matters of literature and art. When they were students Raisa introduced her young husband to the arts, which had scarcely interested him at all. When time permits, both the Gorbachevs are passionate theatregoers. During the season in Moscow, which runs from September to June, they are often to be seen at theatres and concerts. Unlike previous Soviet leaders, Gorbachev takes his wife not only to the classical ballet and opera performances at the Bolshoi or to concerts in the Palace of Congresses at the Kremlin, but also to avant-garde theatres like the Taganka. Mikhail and Raisa sometimes ask to meet the cast after a show, and they are in especially close contact with Mikhail Ulyanov, artistic director of the Vakhtangov Theatre and something of a legend in the Soviet theatrical world.

Ulyanov and other artists sometimes accompany the Gorbachevs on their trips abroad. A large company of performing artists was with the Gorbachevs on their state visit to the USA. It is not, of course, by chance that the Gorbachevs pay close attention to artists and take an active interest in their well-being. Artists are the creative intelligence of any country; they are the social group which can support the politics of *perestroika* in the most attractive way.

8

The Gorbachev Partnership

Many varied, sometimes fantastic notions exist about Raisa's lifestyle, about the everyday habits of the First Lady of the Soviet Union. Some people believe that for the first family of the USSR life is one long holiday, relaxing idly in the lap of luxury. In fact, the rhythm of Raisa's life and work is mainly dictated by her husband's duties, in which she often plays an official role. In an interview published in 1989 in the journal *Reports from the Central Committee of the Soviet Communist Party*, Mikhail Gorbachev said of his wife: 'I have to admit that my duties today are not only a serious, onerous responsibility for me, but also for my family, and I truly value the understanding, support and help I receive from all the members of the family.'

Part of Raisa's time is taken up by her roles as housewife, partner, mother and grandmother. She does not of course do her own shopping or tidy rooms in the President's town residence or the dacha, but running two establishments even with the help of servants is a demanding job. There is much to supervise, and many instructions must be given.

The First Lady of the Soviet Union keeps to a strict timetable. During the eight or nine months of the year when the Gorbachevs are not away from Moscow, either within Russia or abroad, Mikhail Gorbachev's office day begins at 9 am. It takes about forty minutes to drive from the dacha to his office in the Central Committee building, which means he leaves home about 8.15 am.

The Gorbachevs are woken by their staff at 6 am every day,

summer and winter alike. Every morning they must both undergo a medical check-up. Their blood pressure is taken while they are still in bed. Irina, their daughter, and Anatoly, their son-in-law, both qualified doctors, perform this task, if they are sharing the dacha in the summer. Afterwards Raisa has a short swim, drinks a glass of fruit juice, then has breakfast with her husband. On the menu are porridge made with milk, curd cheese, bacon omelettes, semolina, orange juice, coffee with milk or lemon tea (the Gorbachevs prefer German coffee and English tea), and kefir or yoghurt.

After they have discussed the day's schedule, Raisa says goodbye to Mikhail for the rest of the day. She can reach him by telephone at any time, using the state security telephone, but it is an absolute rule that she should do this only in an extreme emergency. After Mikhail has gone, Raisa spends on average half an hour dealing with domestic matters. She goes through the menus of the day with the chef, gives instructions to the housekeeper, pays bills and orders provisions.

Next she turns her attention to correspondence, newspapers and magazines. Every day hundreds of letters arrive, addressed both to Mikhail and Raisa, among them letters from abroad, all of which are sent initially to a special department of the Central Committee of the Soviet Communist Party. The letters are read and analysed and comprehensive reports prepared about the correspondence. Which letters actually reach the Gorbachevs themselves depends on the couple's personal assistants, but, as a rule, letters concerning women's questions are sent on to Raisa, who reckons to spend not less than two hours a day reading correspondence.

Gorbachev sees it as his duty not to become too remote from real life and the problems of ordinary people, which makes Raisa's study of the letters very important to him. She can make him aware in good time in her feminine, intuitive way of the opinions people hold and the criticisms they are making. In this area, as in others, he has complete respect for her judgement. In addition to correspondence, Raisa carefully reads newspapers and magazines, and looks at new books every day. Mikhail does not have the time to keep up fully either with the press or the latest events on the literary scene, and Raisa acts as a kind of information officer. Mikhail Gorbachev of course has his press officers, who evaluate the most important new items for him, but we also know that on media matters and new books he pays particular attention to the briefings he gets from Raisa.

Much of the first half of Raisa's day is thus spent reading. She has her lunch about 2 pm, the usual time in Russia. Mikhail joins her only on his free days; during the week he eats in the dining-room of the Central Committee of the Communist Party. On a public holiday their menu might include fresh fruit juice, salad, vegetables or fish as an appetizer; followed by soup, which might be borscht with lemon wedges and sour cream, or cream of vegetable soup. In summer there is nearly always Raisa's favourite *okroshka*, a chilled soup made of herbs, vegetables and diced meat and flavoured with *kvass*. As a main course they might have chicken or lamb. Mikhail is fond of chicken dishes and vegetable casseroles, curry and curry with fruit. For dessert they eat fruit salad, fresh fruit or fruit mousse – no sweet dishes with a high calorie content. Raisa looks after her figure and believes in eating light, healthy food.

After lunch an hour and a half's rest, if the timetable allows. Raisa then involves herself with her work for the Cultural Foundation, and on some days she has two or three meetings with people from Soviet cultural circles. When Raisa has nothing on her schedule in the afternoon and stays in the dacha, she sometimes takes a little snack, a mixture of fruit, curd cheese, honey and milk, an old recipe supposed to keep the skin smooth and clear. She 'eats for beauty', as they say.

Mikhail seldom arrives home before nine in the evening. Raisa always waits to dine with him. Their usual evening menu is vegetable salad, usually raw vegetables without a sauce, followed by a light fish dish. They like sturgeon, trout, pike and perch. For dessert they have a compote of curd cheese, raisins and dried apricots, or small pastry cases filled with cherries. They drink tea and kefir.

The Gorbachevs do not need a medically prescribed diet, since their own diet is healthy, and, Cossack-style, they eat little bread. Nor do they eat a great deal of meat, potatoes or sauces. Neither of them likes highly-spiced dishes. Once or twice a week food from the West is delivered, most often seafood, and Mikhail loves French cheese.

After supper the Gorbachevs like to take a walk in the garden of their dacha and tell each other about the day's work or discuss problems. They quite often go to the theatre together or to an art exhibition, which means work for the security staff. Several hours before the arrival of the Gorbachevs at the theatre or exhibition hall, the entrances and the auditorium are carefully inspected. Thirty minutes before the show begins, the street in front of the entrance which Mikhail and Raisa Gorbachev will use is cleared of parked cars.

Not just in the Bolshoi Theatre and the Palace of Congresses in the Kremlin, but in every other state theatre, there is a box reserved for the party leader, members of his family and foreign guests of the highest rank. These state boxes in theatres and concert halls are often empty. There are theatres which the leadership never visits, but these boxes must never be made available to anyone else. Usually the state box is to the left of the stage, at a height of about two and a half metres. The Bolshoi Theatre is an exception; the so-called Tsar's Box is down below in the auditorium, directly opposite the stage. In general there are six to eight seats in the front row of a state box and the same number in the row behind. Opposite the state box, to the right of the stage, there is another well-furnished box, the director's box, from which guests of honour invited by the management can watch the performance. These two boxes, which project and indeed tower over the stage, symbolize the all-embracing bureaucratic principle of the exclusivity of the nomenklatura, the separation of the élite from the lower ranks, features which characterized tsarist life and still survive within the Soviet Union.

At the rear of the state box are two richly furnished rooms, with a buffet, so that during the interval or before the curtain goes up guests can have a snack or a glass of tea. When Mikhail Gorbachev goes to a performance directly from the Central Committee offices, he sometimes chooses to eat at the theatre in the interval. Hot dishes are brought ready cooked to the theatre; sometimes they are heated up in the theatre kitchen, otherwise they are kept warm in thermos flasks.

When the Gorbachevs make a private visit to the theatre only one security man usually sits with them in the box. The entrance to the box is guarded, of course, as is the director's entrance, by which the couple enter the theatre. Sometimes the Gorbachevs are joined by Edward Shevardnadze and his wife, or by the Medvedevs. (Vadim Medvedev is a member of the Politburo and responsible for questions of ideology.) A number of young people, who don't actually look like theatregoers, can be seen in the auditorium during the performance. At the interval they slip unobtrusively into the corridors, walk up and down the foyer and stand at every entrance. At the end of the show the waiting convoy of Zil limousines takes the Gorbachevs back to their dacha in Rublev Avenue.

For some nine months of the year, Raisa sees her husband only early in the morning and in the evening – as is the case for the wives of other busy men. There are exceptions, of course, such as public holidays, weekends and the annual four-week leave, which the Gorbachevs spend regularly in Pitsunda, a beautiful old Georgian town on the Black Sea, which has retained its links with the past. The Gorbachevs can be alone here, rest and recuperate. A holiday snap taken outside their house shows them both in relaxed mood: Raisa seems to be making a joke, keeping off the sun with an umbrella. In Miyussera, not far from Pitsunda, a new holiday home was being built for the Gorbachevs, designed in Byzantine style by a leading architect from Tbilisi. Much to the annoyance of Raisa construction has been stopped, following a Congress of People's Deputies which decided that the people are opposed to such ostentation.

During state visits of eminent foreign statesmen to the USSR or on official trips at home and abroad, Raisa Gorbachev often has the chance to be at her husband's side, though the opportunities are strictly dictated by protocol. Official visits account for some twelve weeks in the Gorbachevs' year, and impose considerable strain, but Raisa is intensely supportive of her husband on these occasions, showing enviable energy and vitality.

The reader may have noticed that I have not mentioned in my account of Raisa's timetable how and when the couple find time to meet their friends. The omission is deliberate, for the Gorbachevs choose to live in almost complete isolation, seldom meeting friends and acquaintances privately. Life at the top is a lonely life in a gilded cage, and while Mikhail Gorbachev, preoccupied from morning till night with affairs of state, hardly has time to think of people who were once close to him, the rest of the family, especially Raisa, have to accept the isolation that comes with putting duty before private life.

9

Family Ties

The townhouse and the dacha represent the only places where the Gorbachev family can really count on privacy, places where they can indulge in the give-and-take of family life, relax and put aside their public faces. It is understandable that the Gorbachevs should be so anxious to protect their privacy from outsiders, for they have only a few hours to enjoy the pleasures of ordinary living. Even their closest friends and colleagues from earlier years, people they may well have known since childhood or student days, or in Stavropol, have had to accept that once Mikhail Gorbachev assumed the rank of President, some distancing was inevitable. Relationships changed; terms of intimacy were no longer possible; problems were not the same. Some friends withdrew completely, not wanting to appear to be looking for favours.

The handful of friends that have remained in Mikhail's intimate circle attend his birthday party at the dacha every year. One of them is Yuri Vassilievich Stupin, a friend from Stavropol days, who is now director of the office responsible for allocating sanatoria to Soviet trade unions. Gorbachev himself found this job for Stupin and had him transferred from Kislovodsk to Moscow. Alexander Vladimirovich Vlasov, the former Minister of the Interior, is also one of the regular birthday guests, having been a friend of Gorbachev for more than fifteen years. Others include Edward Shevardnadze and his wife. Shevardnadze always says that he was surprised when Gorbachev suggested during an interval at a party conference that he should become Foreign Minister.

Shevardnadze expressed doubts about his capacities for the job, but Gorbachev replied: 'We've decided already.' The decision has proved to be a wise one.

Gorbachev's sixty-two-year-old cousin and childhood friend, Fedya Vassilievich Rodchenko, son of his mother's sister, is also invited to the party. The Gorbachevs have a warm relationship with Rodchenko, his wife Galia and their daughter Xenia, who works as a criminologist with the Stavropol militia. There is little contact, however, between Mikhail and his forty-one-year-old brother Alexander Sergeyevich Gorbachev, a colonel on the general staff. Alexander, known as Sasha, an enthusiastic guitar-player, is married to Sverta, six years his junior. They have a twenty-year-old daughter, Lena, who is studying at the 2nd Medical Institute in Moscow, where the Gorbachevs' daughter Irina is a tutor. Until the end of 1989 they lived in Odintsovo, twenty minutes from the city, but they now live in central Moscow. Rumours say that the coolness of the relationship has something to do with the fact that Sasha is only Mikhail's half-brother, but there is evidence that Raisa does not get along too happily with her brother-in-law and his wife.

Raisa's affection for her mother-in-law, Maria, appears spontaneously warm. Maria is one of those sturdy, determined women who look you straight in the eye, and is an archetypal Russian mother. She apparently had her grandchild Irina baptised secretly while Mikhail and Raisa were away, seeing the christening as her duty to God. She is also one of those mothers who are direct with their grown-up sons. 'If you have a head full of troubles,' she says to Mikhail, 'go into the field and work them off. That's the way to see things straight.' Her relationship with Raisa is exceptionally strong. 'Son,' she says to Mikhail, 'listen to Raisa, take her advice. She wants the best for you.' I would imagine that Raisa finds no reason to contradict her.

'Baba Manya', Grandma Manya, still works on a smallholding in Privolnoye, where she keeps pigs and chickens. Everyone in the village says she is completely honest. Someone occasionally wants to do the President's mother a small favour, bringing her sugar or something else that is in short supply, but she won't accept gifts, and she insists on paying at the village market. She says she is a Christian believer and will remain one until the day she dies. She flatly refuses to move to Moscow. 'So that they can cremate me there?' she ask cheerfully. In rural Privolnoye the dead are interred in the earth; in Moscow cremation is customary. Some people say that Maria has a closer relationship with her second son, Sasha, than with Mikhail. There was a fierce family row when Sasha wanted to bring her to live with his family in Odintsovo. That was unacceptable to Mikhail. He insisted that if his mother would not come to Moscow to live with him, she must remain in Privolnoye. His mother still lives there, where, I daresay, she belongs; you can't transplant an old tree. She has a modest cottage built with financial help from Mikhail Gorbachev when his father was still alive. The permanent security guard on the house has been intensified since Azerbaijani extremists threatened to wipe out the whole Gorbachev family. Privolnoye is completely out of bounds to Western visitors.

Raisa has an affectionate relationship with her own mother, as well as with Mikhail's mother. 'Baba Shura', Grandma Shura, as Raisa calls her, has lived, since the death of her husband Maxim – who died of cancer of the throat in 1986 – on her own as a pensioner in Krasnodar. She has a small apartment in a five-storey block built in Khrushchev's time and known as a 'Khrushchovka'. The apartment was allocated to Maxim Titorenko on his retirement from work on the Soviet railway. Shura frequently visits her daughter in Moscow, and Raisa travels regularly to Krasnodar. On security grounds Krasnodar is also forbidden to foreigners.

Her two grandchildren, Xenia and Anastasia, have a special place in Raisa's affections. Xenia, born in 1979, is a pupil at the Moscow Special School No. 4, where English is taught as the first foreign language. Anastasia, just three years old, is said to look like her grandfather Mikhail. Her favourite toy is a pale blue furry elephant with a pink trunk, which her grandmother brought her from Paris. In her leisure time Xenia attends the Choreographic School of the Bolshoi Theatre, studying under the famous director Galaptina, whose lessons are given only to children of high-ranking officials. Xenia goes three times a week for two-hour evening sessions. Whenever she possibly can, Raisa picks up Xenia from ballet class, and as she knows the principal of the ballet school well, she often discusses Xenia's progress. She and Xenia leave in a presidential Zil and drive home to supper together.

Raisa is also close to her daughter Irina, whose birthday is the day after Raisa's own. Like her mother she completed her school career as a gold-medal pupil. While she was still at school in Stavropol she met her future husband, Anatoly Verganski, a local Stavropol boy, with whom she later studied medicine at the Medical Institute.

Irina had many admirers, and her mother often had to monitor the number of dance invitations she accepted. Raisa herself is said to have decided that Anatoly was the boy she wanted for Irina. Other admirers were not allowed inside the Gorbachev house. 'I'm glad my daughter didn't fall for a playboy from the city,' Raisa has said. Like his brother Alexei, Anatoly Verganski trained as a heart surgeon. The marriage of Irina and Anatoly in 1977 was an occasion that caught the imagination of the whole of Stavropol. White Volgas were brought out and the wedding celebrations lasted two whole days, the first being given over to the official ceremony and official guests, the second spent with friends. The wedding breakfast was held at the Gorka restaurant.

The wedding photo, taken in traditional style when the ring was being slipped on by the bridegroom, shows a couple who look young to be pledging themselves to a life together. The bridegroom has a baby face, and seems particularly youthful. They look genuinely sweet, and I mean that not just as a wedding-day compliment. There is a rumour that Mikhail spent the second night with the porter, so as not to disturb the two young people, drinking toasts to the couple's health again and again. When I think of Raisa in relation to this rumour, I have to say I simply do not believe it, nor can I imagine that Mikhail Gorbachev would have caroused with a porter at his daughter's wedding, and in Stavropol of all places.

Anatoly Verganski comes from a professional family. His mother is a neuropathologist at the No.8 Polyclinic in Stavropol. His father died young of a tumour of the brain. Doctors have lower status in the Soviet Union than in the West, where the white coat has a certain glamour.

Irina brought to the marriage all the virtues of a dutiful daughter. She was well-educated, and one of the family servants, Yefremova, had taught her the domestic skills of cooking, baking, knitting and sewing. She plays the piano, speaks fluent English and I understand she can talk knowledgeably about art. She seems to be an admirable young woman in every way. Raisa's stimulating intelligence and Mikhail's fatherly affection combined to produce an ideal home atmosphere in which to grow up.

Until the birth of her second daughter, Irina worked at No.2 Medical Institute in Moscow, lecturing on therapy, while Anatoly was for some years an assistant doctor at the Gradski Hospital, whose director, Victor Savelyev, is a specialist in heart surgery. Savelyev's wife is a gynaecologist who numbers Raisa among her patients. The women friends I have in Moscow regard the fact that Raisa Gorbachev is a patient of a gynaecologist as significant. They say she is a modern woman who visits the gynaecologist once a year. When I said I couldn't understand what was so modern about that, they said: 'It's nothing unusual by your standards in the West, but it is unusual by Russian standards.'

They told me that gynaecological treatment as a whole had been made much more difficult in the Soviet Union because of inadequate medical facilities and the prejudices of husbands who forbade their wives to allow a doctor to examine them intimately. Many wives accepted the prohibition, but remained apprehensive about illnesses and unwanted pregnancies. My friends described abortion in the Soviet Union as a horrific event, performed without an anaesthetic, and under conditions which increased the mortality rate. The degree of ignorance on the whole subject remains enormous. Men are not specially interested in 'women's suffering', and apparently male prejudice extends to the government's failure to provide any method of contraception. Raisa would seem to me in this respect a privileged woman, married to a privileged man.

As a student Raisa stayed in close touch with her brother and sister, but they seldom meet today. Her much younger sister Ludmilla studied medicine, married an engineer and had two children, a girl and a boy. The girl is a student at the Academy of Art in Moscow and wants to be a painter. The boy is studying at the Technical High School in Moscow. Ludmilla's marriage is said to be somewhat precarious. Ludmilla practises today as a doctor in Ufa, a city to the west of the Urals, best known, the Russians say, for its degree of environmental pollution, the highest in the Soviet Union. Friends say that Ludmilla seldom visits Raisa in Moscow, and it is difficult for an outsider to say whether it is just the geographical distance that keeps the sisters apart.

Yevgeny Titorenko used to accompany his adolescent sister Raisa to dances, and protect her from over-attentive admirers. Evgeny completed his military service and started at university; like Raisa he entered the philosophy department of Moscow State University. He was writing children's stories and novels, but could not get them published. Raisa says of her brother's writing: 'His stories have a touch of Kafka.' One of his short stories written in 1973, 'Kitomski's Sea', tells of a sailor stationed on the North Sea coast who comes home on leave and falls in love with a girl. They marry, and he goes back to the north to prepare the house for the arrival of his young bride. As he waits for her on the bank of the estuary, the steamer comes into port. He waves to her. Suddenly he sees a mine in the water. He dives in, defuses the mine, saves her and loses his life . . .

Yevgeny Titorenko often relied on his sister Raisa for advice. He married twice and has a son, who did his military service in East Germany. For years Yevgeny has lived alone in Voronezh, and it is said that he underwent a cure for dependence on alcohol in a psychiatric clinic in Orel. There have been occasions when he is reported to have had heated arguments with his sister Raisa. Certainly he has been no help to her in her career.

They say in Moscow that it was Raisa's tragic experience with her brother that prompted her to urge Mikhail to initiate his anti-alcohol campaign, at a time when the consumption of vodka in the Soviet Union had risen to alarming heights. Gorbachev himself may enjoy a drink occasionally, but Raisa is vehemently opposed to alcohol.

Raisa's father, Maxim Titorenko, was buried one summer day in 1986. Almost the whole family assembled for this occasion, and Mikhail attended the funeral in his black suit with a black tie, placing a bunch of red carnations beside the portrait of the dead man. Raisa's mother, in a black outfit with a black lace veil, walked with her head bowed, a white handkerchief in front of her face. Raisa, carrying a spray of red roses, supported her mother. She, too, was dressed in mourning, hardly recognizable in her grief, her face wracked with pain. Raisa's father lay in the open coffin in a white shroud, surrounded by lighted candles, in a typical Soviet funeral ceremony. To the right of the coffin were two rows of chairs, and in the first row sat Mikhail, Raisa and

Raisa's mother; then came Yevgeny, the only mourner in a dark brown suit, and Ludmilla, who looks very like her sister. There were also relatives of Maxim Titorenko from the Ukraine, more colourfully dressed than the other mourners. Behind them sat Irina and her husband Anatoly, Anatoly's mother and Lydia Budyka, Raisa's friend, with her husband Alexander, a colleague of Mikhail Gorbachev's on the Central Committee.

10

The Woman and her Clothes

Whenever I hear Raisa's name in connection with fashion, I have to smile. So much nonsense has been written about her. Hardly a day goes by without one of the popular papers printing some new 'sensation' about her. 'Raisa has fifty couture dresses from Paris designers'; 'Each of her outfits costs at least £3,000'; 'Raisa is a walking advertisement for Cardin or Yves Saint Laurent'; 'The tsar of Russian fashion, Slava Zaitsev, designs for Raisa exclusively.' One columnist contrived to change Slava Zaitsev into a female designer. I can only assume that the journalists are graduates of some college of journalism, writing their features in the office, without the labour of collecting information on the scene. 'The Communist lady with the Parisian chic', they say of Raisa. During her visits to the West, designers watched her closely, critically.

Some praised her understated elegance, others found the mixture of stripes, dots and diamonds in the material of her English-style suit perfectly judged; Karl Lagerfeld, by contrast, thought that her use of gold-threaded fabric suggested a Russian dirndl, better suited to a beer garden than a state visit. He doubted whether you could fairly say that she wore fashions; rather, that she had a wardrobe full of clothes. Whatever their reservations, all the fashion critics agreed that Raisa Gorbachev looked feminine and charming.

I wanted to know more about the Soviet First Lady's approach to fashion and elegance. I therefore went to see Slava Zaitsev, the famous Russian fashion designer, whose avant-garde creations are known in the West as well as in Soviet Russia.

Slava Zaitsev was the subject of a series in *Free World*, a magazine mainly devoted to life in the Soviet Union, over ten years ago. A journalist tried to describe his style to West German readers, emphasizing its avant-garde aspects. The series was not particularly successful in achieving this ambition, and only proved that Russian avant-garde fashion is no more wearable than its Western counterpart. But that was some time ago.

I was lucky to get an interview with Slava Zaitsev. He is so much in demand, he makes appointments six months ahead, and even then he may turn out to be indisposed.

In his white, brightly-lit office Slava came towards me, kissed me, Russian style, on both cheeks and led me to a chair. He said straightaway that he did not design clothes for Raisa, nor did he want to be part of the Gorbachev legend. He has no desire to wear a dark suit (Slava loves white) and he says he wants to design for ordinary people. But he admitted that his dream was for Raisa Gorbachev to open a fashion collection, somewhere in Western Europe, showing his work and that of Valentino. A Zaitsev–Valentino collection presented by Raisa Gorbachev. That is what he would love to happen.

Slava sees himself not simply as someone who makes clothes, but as an artist. Since 1978 he has been developing official designs for a new kind of work clothing for the general public: men and women, even children – an exemplary socialist concept. Like so many things in Russia, the Institute where he works is shabby and neglected, and constrained by the universal economic shortages. Fabrics, thread, zip fasteners, sewing machines and other labour-saving equipment, everything is in short supply, which naturally handicaps creativity. Under such circumstances, can there ever be a Karl Lagerfeld or an Yves Saint Laurent in the Soviet Union? Slava in reply quotes his personal motto: 'Out of nothing – everything.'

I sit in my armchair as Slava walks up and down, gesticulating with his beautiful, expressive hands, which he uses all the time when talking. Life is for living, he says, and within him is joy, energy, optimism. He believes in *perestroika*. Everything will turn out well. 'When Gorbachev took over this country it was in a catastrophic state. He may be only one man, but people in the Soviet Union are already friendlier and more human with each other. Is that a small thing?' he asks. Slava opened the State Fashion House, a kind of fashion atelier for everybody, in 1982, and he is Director of the Institute of Fashion. People working in the Institute appointed him themselves, first going on strike, then electing him. His first official duty as director was to choose the colour of the house. He chose pure white. That was just the beginning. Now he has about four hundred people working with him.

He is committed to the concept of the Soviet professional woman, and believes she needs the help of his talent if she is going to look well-dressed at work and elegant when she goes out in the evening. He gives the situation much thought, looks at women when they tell him their troubles, which they want to disguise by wearing a stunning dress. Clothes can be a psychological tonic, as we all know. In his philosophy of life it is not money that counts. He has no desire to try to satisfy a host of clients, which would cramp his creativity, for, as he says: 'Out of nothing – everything.'

Because Slava does not design clothes for Raisa, it does not follow that he has no designer's image of her, no perception of how he would like to dress her. The fact remains they have never actually met. 'We are perhaps too complicated for each other,' says Zaitsev, fluttering his hands. 'It can happen. You get to know people and you have to be careful, in case you are mutually destructive.' Arrangements have twice been made for him to meet Raisa Gorbachev, once at the French Embassy, when Yves Saint Laurent was presenting his collection, and the second time at the first night of *Sophisticated Lady* at a Russian theatre. On both occasions Slava says he did not have the time to keep to the arrangement.

As a Soviet arbiter of fashion, Slava sees Raisa in a highly favourable light: trim figure, well-proportioned, with slim legs and, most importantly, the desire to look attractive. Raisa Gorbachev is for him a real woman, and he only regrets that in fashion she does not always get the best advice. Such a shame! He has no time, and she wafts around in outfits that don't suit her. I find this all a bit ridiculous. Zaitsev does not, but says that unfortunately it is not in his power to change things, which I can well believe. He says no to the queen, and then *he* expects *her* to talk him round.

'Have you ever designed clothes for Irina, Raisa's daughter?' I asked.

'I am a couturier, not a celebrity-hunter,' Zaitsev replied curtly, adding dreamily, 'when I was young, I designed clothes for Raisa Gorbachev all the time, without ever telling her. I was fascinated by her hair. It inspired me, the colour, the richness, the possibilities of starting something.'

Slava has moved a long way from such fantasies. He designs after examining the figure of a woman with detachment and discussing things with her. Only when he has really studied a woman's shape, especially her hips – often a problem for Russian women – do ideas come to him, so that he can advise clients about their mistakes and what they ought to wear in order to look good. But he remains the kind of person who likes to play games. 'Just imagine if Raisa came in and said: "Mr Zaitsev" – she wouldn't say Slava, not Raisa – "I need a dinner dress." I would have to think about this in a practical way,' he went on, 'I would first need to know how much fabric I could use. So often wives of Soviet officials come with the minimum amount of dress material. Possibly their husbands didn't have the foreign currency to buy more, possibly they had the length of fabric as a gift. Shortage of material hurts my powers of invention.' Then Slava waved his hands over his papers. 'I would dress the Tsarina Raisa with her glowing chestnut hair [always the hair] in a straight little black dress, about knee-length, softly tailored, interwoven with pearly threads, glittering black stockings, high heels – and that for me would be my "Raisa *Glasnost*" design.'

Slava, now in full flow, suggests that in the wake of *perestroika* Soviet women will take centre stage, become more open, more ambitious, live for themselves, know what they want to do and actually do it. At the moment they play only the roles society has assigned to them.

I do not, of course, need to ask the real reason why he does not make clothes for Raisa. Slava knows this perfectly well. He admits frankly that he is not serious, not earnest enough for the First Lady of the land. In his view, he behaves like an eager small boy wanting to lead his own unconventional life, not wanting to conform or be told which clothes he should design. He doesn't like women simply to order a dinner dress. He prefers women who come to him and say: 'Look at me, Mr Zaitsev, what can be done with me? I would like to start a new life.' His aim is to create new personalities, not clothes for special occasions. The sketches that Zaitsev made as we were talking are in front of me on the table. They show lovely, supple bodies, slim, graceful, a touch of Art Nouveau, taut, loose, fluent, inventive. We could have been in a small café in Paris instead of in Moscow, but Slava is Russian and belongs to Moscow.

My interview with Slava Zaitsev, interesting as it had been, had not provided me with an answer to the question: Who is actually responsible for the First Lady's clothes? I decided to ask people in Stavropol, where Raisa lived for twenty-three years. Pictures of Raisa as a young woman suggested that even then she was fashion-conscious. It was often some small detail, nothing expensive or ostentatious, which enabled her to stand out from her plainly dressed companions and pinpointed the beginnings of a style of her own. She was, after all, the woman student in Moscow who wore a winter coat with a little fur collar.

In Stavropol Raisa's clothes were made by a local dressmaker, Sonya Vasilievna Karetnikova. Mrs Karetnikova made dresses for all the women in the Gorbachev household, including Irina's wedding dress. When I visited her, she searched through a wooden chest and took out Irina's wedding photographs. 'I also made Raisa Gorbachev's dress for Irina's wedding,' she said. 'The mother of the bride must look attractive. I remember that while we were trying things on, Mikhail lay down on a couch. He had just come back from an official trip and he had a headache. We fitted the dress on, and I said to Raisa: "This dress is my wedding present." Raisa looked wonderful in it, but she said, "No, it's too expensive a gift." I insisted she should have it, otherwise, I said, I would take it back home. At this point Mikhail opened his eyes and looked fondly at Raisa, saying "Ah, Sakhar ["sugar" in Russian], you've never had a dress like that, and how beautiful you look"!' 'Sakhar' is Mikhail's pet name for Raisa, and it goes back to their student days. Raisa often used to wear Mikhail's leather jacket, and even in those days she liked to give the orders, so that Mikhail also calls her jokingly his 'Commissar'.

Mrs Karetnikova was eloquent on the subject of Raisa and Mikhail. 'He loves her so much,' she said. 'Once, at the end of the 1960s as I remember, Mikhail went to Italy and spent all his money on silver jewellery to bring back for Raisa. I made her a

141

silver cocktail dress, and she later wore it all for their silver wedding. She looked marvellous.'

Sonya speaks of all this with deep personal satisfaction. You feel that a genuine human relationship still exists between her and Raisa. She recalled how she used to say: 'Bring me three hundred roubles and I will make you a fantastic dress.' Raisa would bring the roubles, leaving Sonya Karetnikova to choose the pattern and the material and make the dress, so that she would only have to turn up for the fitting.

'When she was choosing designer clothes, too, I had to decide,' Sonya Karetnikova says proudly. 'She always said, you, Sonya, you have the last word, shall I take it or not?' Even in fashion-conscious Italy, Sonya's clothes were a success. The Gorbachevs were there for a Communist Party celebration, and when their escort called Raisa 'Signora Grazia' (the Lady with the Graces), Raisa modestly gave credit for this compliment on her appearance to Sonya Karetnikova and her collection. 'That isn't so,' Sonya says. 'What makes the difference to clothes is the person inside them and the way clothes are worn. Raisa knows how to wear clothes. She makes them come alive.'

But who supervises Raisa's wardrobe in Moscow today? I discovered that she – like other wives in the highest ranks of the nomenklatura – orders from a catalogue, which enables her to obtain copies of Dior, Claude Montana, Chanel and other labels. Raisa orders what appeals to her, without necessarily knowing the name of the designer, since the clothes are not labelled. She always attends the annual Festival of Fashion in Moscow, at which fashion houses from all over the Soviet Union show their collections. If she sees something she likes, she may order straight from the catwalk. On her trips abroad she usually manages to visit couturiers and fashion shows. In 1986, for instance, on a state visit to East Germany, she moved outside the official programme to go shopping privately in a fashion boutique for herself and her daughter. The West has long been conscious of her interest in fashion, and the hosts responsible for her programme on overseas visits always enable her to meet their country's top fashion designers. On these occasions she sometimes receives presents, which she generally passes on to her daughter, Irina, for high-fashion clothes do not always suit her personal style, which is somewhat conservative.

Raisa's enthusiasm for fashion has naturally had an effect within the Soviet Union, where she is frequently urging consumer industries to produce goods faster, more efficiently, and in clothing, above all, more fashionably designed. There is, unfortunately, still a wide gap between desire and reality, and it will probably be a long time before the average Russian woman can buy clothes like Raisa's.

A Russian friend told me that Raisa did not buy all her clothes from the catalogue, and promised to introduce me to the woman who is currently the First Lady's chief fashion adviser and also designs some of her clothes. 'I hope it wasn't too difficult a journey for you,' said Tamara Konstantinova Makeyeva, who does not look her sixty years, and is the designer my friend had mentioned. She was willing to talk to me, the first time she has talked to any observer, about her famous client.

It had not been the easiest of journeys to visit Mrs Makeyeva. It had taken me through beautiful Russian towns – Rostov, Veliki and Yaroslavl, all beside the Volga – to the village of Shilikova, near the Volga town of Kostroma, where Mrs Makeyeva has her private dacha. She spends two months in the summer here with her family. She is proud of the fact that the great Russian dramatist Ostrovsky had his country estate in Shilikova. Her husband is an actor at the Mossovet Theatre in Moscow, while she herself works in the state House of Fashion near the Kuznetski Bridge, which differs from the fashion house directed by Slava Zaitsev in its more conservative attitude to colour and style. Tamara Makeyeva and Zaitsev worked together for fifteen years sharing a studio, which is probably the only thing the two designers have in common today.

Tamara Makeyeva met Raisa some eight years ago. Friends from the Mossovet Theatre brought them together, suggesting that Makeyeva should design a dress for Gorbachev's wife. Her first design was a dark blue suit, rather severe in cut, with two skirts, one maxi-skirt and one calf-length, and a short jacket. There was also a white blouse for parties. When Raisa moved into the Kremlin with her husband, she sought out Mrs Makeyeva, made arrangements to meet, and since then Tamara Makeyeva has been mainly responsible for Raisa Gorbachev's wardrobe. They get along easily on a personal level, and Raisa gives Mrs Makeyeva a reasonably free hand in designing her clothes. Their meetings seldom last less than two hours. While the two women discuss designs or the fit of a dress, herbal tea is served, a mixture of blackcurrant, limeflower and dried mint, 'all from the forest near my dacha,' says Mrs Makeyeva, who always returns to Moscow from Shilikova with a year's supply.

The designer prepares carefully for her sessions with Raisa, studying international fashion trends in Rome, Paris, London and Düsseldorf from fashion magazines. When both women have agreed on a design, Galina Kopolova, Mrs Makeyeva's assistant, enters the picture. It is her job to lay out materials suitable for the design, cut the pattern, and eventually sew the dress for the first fitting. A shortlist is drawn up from the models that are liked. The women reach the final decision quite alone. I have never heard of Mikhail Gorbachev interfering in matters of his wife's wardrobe. A few days after a visit to Mrs Makeyeva, Raisa can be seen and admired in a new dress.

Raisa's feeling for colour is largely influenced by her emotional mood, according to Mrs Makeyeva. As a rule she prefers warm, bright colours, especially red, but sometimes she will decide on an unobtrusive grey. Everything has to match. She is very particular about that. Mrs Makeyeva is ecstatic about the marvellous way Raisa helps Soviet fashion. 'She is the first General Secretary's wife who dresses well and shows the world how good a Russian woman can look,' she says. Her meetings with Raisa are full of tension and excitement, for Mrs Makeyeva, who is not only ambitious to satisfy Raisa's expectations but wants to be accepted on equal terms with Westerners as a contemporary fashion designer, hopes that Raisa Gorbachev will make her name known in the wider world. Plainly Mrs Makeyeva doesn't read West European magazines. She would be disappointed by the journalists' ignorance; she would find the names of Cardin, Lagerfeld and Dior, but not her own.

I asked her what sort of fabrics she provided for Raisa and was told they came mainly from outside the Soviet Union, and were generally imported from France or England, where Mrs Makeyeva believes the finest materials are produced. She does, however, occasionally use Russian-made fabrics.

Mrs Makeyeva takes an understandable pride in having as a client the first Soviet leader's wife to take an interest in fashion at an informed and intelligent level. She would like other Soviet wives to follow Raisa's example, but is realistic enough to know that few Soviet women enjoy Raisa's advantages. Nevertheless, she believes that Soviet women could pay more attention to their appearance and make more of themselves. 'That need not cost a great deal of money,' she added. 'Small details can make a huge improvement.'

Over the years a friendly relationship has grown up between the two women. Whenever she visits the designer Raisa takes presents for Mrs Makeyeva's grandchildren: brightly-coloured children's books, rubber balls, chewing gum, or other things she knows will please small children. But the two months in the summer that Mrs Makeyeva spends in her dacha belong to her and to her alone. Raisa never so much as phones her up during this period, accepting that the time is, as it were, sacrosanct.

A few days after our interview Mrs Makeyeva was due to celebrate her sixtieth birthday. Every year she receives a birthday bouquet from the First Lady of the Kremlin, and she knew that this year it would be a bigger one to mark the special occasion. 'Raisa's love of giving presents is one of the strongest traits in her character,' said Mrs Makeyeva.

Another aspect of Raisa's appearance interested me. Who deals with her hair and make-up? Who brings out those stunning chestnut-brown highlights in her hair and cares for the porcelain quality of her skin? By chance I met Boris Gusiyev, who had been Raisa's hairdresser until 1985 and had advised her on make-up before Mikhail Gorbachev became General Secretary. Boris Gusiyev was working at the relevant time in the Moscow Hair Research Institute. Anyone who went to the Institute had to fill in a questionnaire with personal details, and after each consultation the specialist wrote down for the records suggestions he had made. Gusiyev told me that the first time Raisa visited there she came with a woman friend, a professor of philosophy. She then came regularly two or three times a month, making her appointments by phone. Raisa did not always follow Gusiyev's advice, often arriving with her own clear idea of what she wanted done. He soon learned from his famous client that Mikhail liked Raisa's hair to have a hint of romance about it, and it is no secret that her hair is tinted with henna. As for her make-up, Gusiyev said that she attached great importance to a good, usually cream-coloured foundation. Unlike the majority of Russian women, who prefer harsh, bright lipstick, Raisa chooses delicate rosy pinks.

Raisa Gorbachev is not the only member of her family who has consulted Gusiyev. One day he was asked to look at her granddaughter's hair, which was not growing as Xenia would have liked. He was taken by car to Alexei Tolstoy Street, where Irina and Xenia were waiting for him. Both were apparently satisfied by Gusiyev's advice, for after further consultations and styling sessions Xenia stopped worrying about her hair.

Inevitably Gusiyev and Raisa discussed things other than hair-styles and make-up. Their conversations were far from the usual 'hairdresser's gossip'. They talked mainly about art and culture, Gusiyev said, and from the tone and tenor of my discussions with him I know he has cultured tastes. He is a man with no appetite for scandal or headlines, but with a deep love of literature. As if he felt he had to prove the point to me, he quoted from a poem written in the winter of 1916 by the famous Russian poet Anna Akhmatova:

There are words you must say only once,

Once you have spoken them you have surrendered.
The heavens rising into the blue
Are inexhaustible . . .

As he recited the lines he stood up, and went over to his bookcase to take out a slim volume, *Poems of Akhmatova*. I thought at first he was going to read another poem, but he pressed the book into my hand for me to see. 'Raisa herself gave me this book as a present,' he said. 'She also gave me other books of poetry by Akhmatova. We share an enthusiasm for her poetry.

'Raisa is a pleasant, responsive woman,' Boris went on. 'She knows what her position demands of her and she is always well-groomed. She cares about her appearance, keeps slim and always dresses well. She knows exactly what she wants. She loves to change her hairstyle, sometimes severe, sometimes feminine, but always right for the occasion.'

Gusiyev is still appalled at the memory of the time he kept Raisa waiting, as if she were just another client. He had filled in the form as usual about Raisa's hair and had then become so involved in his work with other clients he forgot about his appoint-ment with her. It was only when he saw Raisa's face that he realized who he had kept waiting. Raisa herself was very relaxed about it, saying: 'I respect your principles.' His superiors were, however, livid with him for having kept the wife of the youngest member of the Central Committee, Mikhail Gorbachev, waiting.

Today Raisa has a different hairdresser, Tatiana, who also deals with her make-up and accompanies her on trips abroad. Tatiana used to work with Boris Gusiyev at the Hair Research Institute. Gusiyev stopped working for Raisa Gorbachev in 1985 for what he describes as 'personal reasons', and today is employed in a private hairdressing salon, Ginseng, in Moscow, where, he says, he earns good money. I was not allowed to question Tatiana, who had signed an undertaking when she took the job to reveal no details about it to outsiders.

Raisa's elegance and interest in fashion inspire ambivalent feelings in the Soviet Union, especially among women. You find evidence of these feelings in the newspapers, and people, when questioned, give subjective views on her. Some women regard Raisa's outfits as signalling what they ought to wear, silk or cotton, polka dots or large motifs. She is a model for Soviet dressmakers to follow.

Others take a malicious line, saying that Raisa throws money out of the window and projects a false image of Soviet women. 'Our women are not like her,' said Pavel, a Moscow acquaintance of mine. 'I would go crazy with someone like her.'

'Why like her?' I asked.

He replied, 'It isn't as if it's her own money she's spending. We have to pay for everything. She ought to wear the kind of gear we wear, then people in America would realize what's really lacking in Russia.'

11

Passport to Perestroika

The journeys of the Gorbachevs are familiar to the world. The Soviet couple are surrounded by an eager media pack whenever they disembark at an international airport. Raisa inspires headlines wherever she goes, cast as 'The First Lady of the Eastern Bloc', 'The Red Tsarina', 'Promoter of Perestroika', or whatever catchpenny phrase the media can dream up.

Lydia Budyka says that Raisa is passionately keen on travel. 'Wherever Raisa goes, she visits art galleries and museums, and attends as many concerts and theatres as possible. She greatly enjoys music, books and paintings, for culture is what impresses her most. She doesn't go shopping. What she brings back are her impressions of a country's culture and its people.'

Lydia may be right about the culture, but I just can't accept what she says about shopping. I believe this claim springs from a particularly Soviet kind of prudery, which thinks it dishonourable to show too much regard for material things. Soviet citizens are notoriously short of material things, and one of the objectives of the Gorbachev journeys is to gain assistance in remedying the shortages, but the prudery persists.

It is only natural that Raisa should go shopping. In 1984, before Mikhail Gorbachev became General Secretary, she is known to have been excited by some jewellery she saw in London. Raisa asked Margaret Thatcher where she had bought her diamond earrings. Mrs Thatcher recommended her jeweller, Cartier, advising Raisa to insist on a reasonable price, and newspaper reports described a charming pair of earrings later bought for about £1000, considered a reasonable price.

Raisa gathered other impressions in London. While her husband was holding discussions with the British Prime Minister, Raisa was shown around 10 Downing Street. She noticed approvingly the free and informal way members of the Prime Minister's staff talked to her about the official residence, telling her anecdotes about the paintings on the walls and details such as the number of crystals in a splendid chandelier, or the history behind the different rooms. All this was new to Raisa, and since this was one of her first trips abroad with a Soviet delegation and she had few official engagements, she could absorb everything with a free mind.

When Mikhail Gorbachev became General Secretary in 1985, he had to assume a higher profile internationally, and his wife's engagements multiplied and became more formal in style. Her open, easy attitude vanished in the strict organization of her programme, which was now arranged to relate to her husband's timetable of official meetings and discussions. Her personal tastes were not a significant factor in fixing her schedules. Cultural events were no longer of paramount importance, having to yield to official occasions which created photo opportunities. Tea with the head of state's wife, receptions with her husband and their host and hostess.

Raisa Gorbachev was now perpetually under the scrutiny of the media, her every move observed. I have noticed myself one gesture she regularly makes, which could perhaps be a gesture of embarrassment, dating back to when she wore her hair in a coil of plaits round her head. She pushes her hair back from her forehead and feels with her hand along the nape of her neck. As a naturally neat and tidy person, she would always have checked that there were no loose strands.

When the President and his wife leave on a trip abroad, the entire Politburo is traditionally at Vnukovo Airport, one of Moscow's major airports, to witness the takeoff. The routine before 1985 was that Raisa would board the aircraft by a side entrance, separately from her husband, without any fuss and unrecorded by the television cameras. In 1986 Mikhail decided that he and his wife would board the plane together, visible to all. The President has an Ilyushin 62 at his disposal for long flights. For shorter journeys he generally uses a Tupolev. The

Soviet Ministry of Civil Aviation has a department dealing solely with the transportation of state and party leadership. It has a fleet of between twenty and twenty-five Ilyushins and 134 Tupolevs under its control. Two aircraft are in a state of readiness for a presidential call day and night. They are comfortably furnished, with a private compartment for Mikhail, where he can work, eat and sleep. The aeroplanes also have a conference room holding about thirty people, with a news communications centre, the hotline red telephone for nuclear alerts, and places for stenographers. The doctors and security men who accompany Mikhail and Raisa on their travels have separate cabins, and there is, of course, a kitchen, a cold store and a rest room for the crew.

The presidential aircraft has carefully selected crews, highly qualified for their technical jobs and positively vetted to warrant the highest security grading. At least three stewardesses accompany the President and his wife.

At least ten days before Mikhail and Raisa arrive in a foreign country, the advance guard of their security section leaves the Soviet Union to plan security for the visit, in cooperation with their opposite numbers in the host country. They work out routes and agree plans, so that there will be no hitches during the actual visit. Some five days ahead of the Gorbachevs, Gennady Gerasimov, the chief Soviet spokesman, and the Soviet media corps arrive, followed two days later by the Zil chauffeurs and their fleet of limousines, which meet President Gorbachev and his wife Raisa, elegant and photogenic, as they come down the aircraft steps.

The President is always accompanied by a group of between ten and twenty who travel with him in the aircraft, a delegation chosen in the context of a particular visit. Frau Freundlich, German-born, travelled with the Gorbachevs on the visit to West Germany, when the problem of resettlement of German-born citizens in Russia was high on the agenda. Directors of principal Soviet museums are often in the group. Raisa's hairdresser, Tatiana, and a personal 'lady in waiting' are in attendance on every trip.

The security forces are also always there. Like her husband, Raisa Gorbachev has a personal security guard on every overseas journey, and one can always spot seven or eight officers from the KGB Group 5 never more than five metres away from her. Raisa and Mikhail do not make any move abroad that has not been approved by security officers of the KGB and the host country, who are understandably anxious whenever Mikhail and Raisa decide spontaneously to get out of the official limousine to go walkabout. Tension is at maximum level, for who knows what dangers lurk behind a smiling face in the crowd?

In his five years as General Secretary, Mikhail and his wife have visited over thirty foreign countries, inspiring a number of jokes in Moscow. 'What is the difference between the Moscow Olympics and the Congress of People's Deputies?' (The Congress of People's Deputies took place in the spring of 1989, just before Mikhail and Raisa left for a state visit to West Germany. The publicity symbol mascot of the Olympics was an inflatable bear named 'Misha', which also happens to be Gorbachev's nickname.) The answer: 'At the Olympics Misha had to be inflated to fly away. At the Congress Misha inflated himself to fly away.' The political implication was that he was escaping from troubles at home.

Another story which went the rounds had Mikhail and Raisa lying in an imperial bed on a state visit to France. Mikhail says to Raisa: 'Did you ever imagine you would one day be sleeping with a General Secretary?' She replies: 'Did you ever imagine you would be sleeping with a General Secretary's wife?' Raisa Gorbachev knows who she is.

Raisa Gorbachev demonstrates to the world a new, modern image of the Soviet woman, which owes something to fashion, make-up and hairstyle, but more to her education, self-assurance and sense of her own worth, which she projects impressively. She might not always make friends, but she undoubtedly makes an impact. She has an effect on the women back home in the Soviet Union, doing heavy work like men, and still, as the Russians say, keeping an eye on the cooking-pot. Her speeches abroad remind the world of the Soviet women deprived by the Great Patriotic War of the chances of love and a family of their own. She uses them to illustrate her belief that it is women who suffer most in war and who must try not just to preserve peace, but to instigate it. The sharpest criticism of Raisa comes in my experience from Russian émigré women, for instance those living in the USA. They know what Russia was like in the past and are aware of the status of Soviet women today. 'Raisa is one of those who likes to be on the gravy train,' they say maliciously.

Criticisms like that do not dent her self-confidence. She continues to display her literary knowledge, sometimes when nobody asks her to do so. In Iceland she talked of reading Halldor Laxness, in England and America her press officers issued her opinions on Charles Dickens and J. D. Salinger. In France she went to exhibitions of Monet, Renoir and Van Gogh and gave little lectures to those around on the artists and their significance in the world. She is particularly forthcoming about Picasso's painting and emphasizes that it is the Soviet people who have taken his dove of peace to heart.

Raisa doesn't believe in hiding her learning under a bushel, which can in itself make an impression on people. When President Reagan's wife, Nancy, was showing her round the White House in Washington, Raisa's endless questions about the history of its interior so unnerved the American First Lady that she had to send for a White House guide who could keep pace with Raisa's wide-ranging knowledge.

In her autobiography, *My Turn*, Nancy Reagan makes no secret of her antipathy for Raisa. 'When she came to tea in Geneva that first day, she struck me as a woman who expected to be deferred to. When she didn't like the chair she was seated in, she snapped her fingers to summon her KGB guards, who promptly moved her to another chair. After sitting in the new spot for a couple of minutes, she decided she didn't like that one either, so she snapped her fingers and they moved her again. I couldn't believe it. I had met First Ladies, princesses and queens, but I had never seen anybody act this way.'

Raisa certainly didn't make things easy for Nancy. One example was the summit meeting at Reykjavik. Nancy apparently thought the summit was to be just a meeting between the heads of state of America and Russia, and therefore did not accompany Ronald Reagan. She then had to watch on television as the Soviet First Lady turned it into the Raisa show. Raisa commented on Nancy's absence with sympathy and bafflement: 'Perhaps she isn't well, or perhaps she has something else to do.' This calculated compassion left Nancy Reagan watching the screen in fury, complaining about the unfairness of a woman she saw as a rival for international attention.

The Nancy chapter is, of course, now closed. Raisa's relationship with Barbara Bush can only be an improvement on the one she had with Nancy Reagan, though the Malta Summit in December 1989 had moments of discord. Once again, the First Lady of America had stayed at home, while the First Lady of the Soviet Union accompanied her husband. Raisa remained in the background at first, but not for long. She explained to waiting journalists: 'The President isn't here, sorry,' referring to President Bush, who, because the sea was so stormy, couln't get over to the Soviet ship. In Soviet diplomatic circles it was rumoured that Raisa listened in an adjoining room to the negotiations between Gorbachev and George Bush, to enable her to give Gorbachev her thoughts on how the follow-up discussions should advance.

On the historic visit to the Pope in December 1989, Raisa again broke with convention. In contrast to Nancy Reagan and Britain's Princess of Wales, she arrived at the Vatican without the customary black mantilla, wearing a bright red suit, which announced her as the First Lady of the Communist world. Raisa is not a Christian and Mikhail Gorbachev says of his wife: 'She is the atheist of the two of us, but she speaks of the Pope with great reverence, and admits that the radiance of his personality fascinated her greatly, something she did not expect.'

In the Soviet Union there is, I found, mounting criticism of what is regarded as Raisa's insensitivity during public appearances. While her husband is perpetually immersed in crises, such as Lithuania and other nationalist pressures, Raisa stands beside him in public, elegant in mink or sable. When he argues fiercely with workers, she seems to smile or make some remark to the women surrounding her. Whether in this way she helps her husband, or stimulates opposition, is an open question.

In the autumn of 1989 the Gorbachevs visited 'Perestroika's secret weapon', Finland, where a visit to a school was, as usual, on the agenda. The visit was shown on Soviet television, and Soviet women reacted crossly when Raisa asked children, who had only been learning the language for two weeks, what they could say in Russian. 'They're not robots,' was the comment.

When Raisa Gorbachev, then unknown outside Russia, appeared for the first time abroad as First Lady of the Soviet Union in Geneva in 1985, all the cameras focused on her, everyone watched to see how she was dressed. She literally stole the media show from her husband. In the years that followed, in which

Mikhail Gorbachev established himself as a catalyst for change in world politics, the interest of the Western public in his wife has shown no sign of fading. The Soviet press, which previously had barely acknowledged the existence of the wife of a General Secretary, decided to project the Gorbachevs as a couple; the word 'mir' means 'peace' in Russian, so you have M for Mikhail, I ('and' in Russian) and R for Raisa, adding up to 'mir'. On visits to countries in the eastern bloc, for instance, to Czechoslovakia or East Germany, Raisa would be pictured in press photographs walking one step behind her husband. In those countries Raisa ranked as Mikhail Gorbachev's wife, and not as First Lady of the Soviet Union.

At the 1987 summit meeting in Washington, DC, I finally met Raisa Gorbachev in person. I was one of a small band of journalists booked into the Madison Hotel where the main Soviet delegation, which included Edward Shevardnadze, the Foreign Minister, and his wife, was staying. The hotel stands directly behind the Soviet Embassy, which was under heavy CIA guard, for Mikhail Gorbachev and his wife were staying there.

I was lucky enough to be invited to a reception given by Raisa Gorbachev in the Soviet Embassy for Russians living abroad. I had only just entered the reception room when security officers moved me back, fortunately close to the door through which Raisa would enter. She came in, wearing her favourite red Makeyeva dress, smiled at me, noticed I was pregnant and asked me in a friendly way when the baby was due. Once we had started a conversation, I found her easy to talk to. We talked about Pushkin, about her love of nature, and my personal hope that *perestroika* would make life simpler for journalists in the Soviet Union. I handed her a badge with 'I like Gorby' on it, which seemed to please her, but she refused to be photographed wearing it. She eventually wished me success in my work and said goodbye pleasantly with a warm handshake, ending a friendly conversation.

I also met Raisa Gorbachev on her trip to Cuba in April 1989. She arrived in Cuba in a pale blue dress designed by Makeyeva, the same one, in fact, that she had worn on her trip to India. She came down the aircraft gangway bare-legged, which was unconventional, but it was warm in Havana, almost 30 degrees, and it had been snowing when the Gorbachevs left Moscow.

When the official party had left the airport, driving past a crowd of banner-waving, celebrating people, the Aeroflot jet was unloaded, enabling one to see that Raisa had a white hatbox, nine green plastic clothes bags and five leather suitcases for the Cuban visit. The Gorbachevs stayed in Lajito, the country house of a former film producer who had been dispossessed by the Cuban government; for their visit new king-size beds were imported from Costa Rica.

One of the high points of Raisa's personal programme was a visit to the former home of Ernest Hemingway, now a Hemingway museum. When Raisa was asked, as she toured the house, whether she had read any Hemingway, she seemed astonished. Everybody must have read Hemingway, her look implied. One American journalist persisted in asking her whether she agreed with Hemingway's views on women, that they ought to be wives and mistresses and nothing else. She finally turned to the reporter to say acidly: 'There are some questions that are so crass they are not worth answering.' Raisa wrote in the museum visitors' book: 'I am happy that I have been able to visit the house where the great writer and humanist Hemingway lived and worked.'

There was a press corps rumour that Raisa also wanted to visit the Mochito Bar, where Hemingway sat evening after evening. The 'Hemingway cocktail' is still served there, but the visit was vetoed on security grounds. They said that Raisa consoled herself with a Hemingway cocktail specially mixed at the villa, but in fact she seldom drinks at all.

In Cuba Raisa visited a children's home run by the Ministry of the Interior. The little girls, all under six, were highly excited. Outside the home Raisa was greeted by a small group of Young Pioneers, who recited their little poems thanking her for coming and bidding her welcome. Raisa assured the Cuban children that the Soviet people sent their best wishes to them, as did Mikhail Gorbachev. She shook their hands, raising their fingers high as if in a ritual, and thanked them for their welcome. The children presented Raisa with a box of chocolates and a red rose. She had brought presents for them, little Russian dolls. All the rooms were brightly decorated, all the little girls in their Sunday best. But a Cuban journalist remarked to me: 'Things will all go back to normal tomorrow. As soon as Raisa's back is turned, the children will be back in their usual squalor.' Raisa carried through the visit with the patience, affection and kindness she always shows to children. She visited the smaller ones in their bedroom – the home takes babies as young as six weeks – and insisted that the press should wait outside, so that the children would not be woken up. On her visit to West Germany she had already impressed people that she was a good mother and grandmother.

On the last day of her Cuban tour journalists waited in vain for Raisa to make her scheduled visit to the Museum of Fine Arts, but she had preferred, apparently on impulse, to visit the Museum of the Revolution without the media in attendance. These sudden alterations in her programme do occur; she may cut visits short or even cancel an appointment, simply saying, 'That's it. Finished. I'm tired.' For that reason it isn't always easy to plan a programme for her. Some West German diplomats said the most difficult part of planning for the Gorbachevs' visit to West Germany was arranging a programme for Raisa Gorbachev, largely because she had her own definite ideas about it. For instance, they proposed to stage a special show for her in the Fashion House, a centre for ready-to-wear clothing in Düsseldorf, but Raisa's concern for fashion had been the subject of criticism in the Soviet Union so she struck this suggestion off the list.

From 5–8 October 1989 I had the opportunity to watch Raisa during a trip to East Berlin. She stayed in the Schloss Nieder-schönhausen in the Pankov district, and on the last day of her visit she went to see the Zeiss Planetarium. In contrast to her previous visits to the German Democratic Republic there were no cheering crowds – only a handful of people, among them a couple of Young Pioneers and one or two girls from the Communist Youth Organization waiting outside the Planetarium. East German security men in civilian clothes were posted every two metres along the route, leaving little room or encouragement for ordinary East Germans to watch the cavalcade of black limousines arrive for the visit, which was not announced in the East German newspapers. A smiling Raisa stepped from a Zil to be greeted by the director of the planetarium.

Erwin, an East German factory worker who admires Raisa, stands, looking slightly embarrassed, with three wilting red roses in his hand. He tells me his wife is Russian and looks like Raisa, and he hopes that the Gorbachevs will bring *glasnost* and *perestroika* to East Germany. A mother carrying a ten-month-old baby,

157

Sandra, manages to push through to Raisa, and when the baby stretches out her hand Raisa asks: 'Would you let me hold you for a minute?' The baby tries to grab her black crocodile handbag. Raisa smiles, looking for the moment the picture of the proud grandmother: 'Come, my little diplomat, come and see what your aunt from Moscow has brought you,' she says, opening her handbag to take out a little box of pralines, wrapped in floral paper. Raisa says the baby reminds her of her granddaughter Anastasia, who also likes to grab at everything. She gives her bag to the director of the planetarium to hold. The baby won't let go of Raisa. 'Our little diplomat is never satisfied.' says Raisa. 'Let's look in the bag again and see if we can find something to play with.' When she asks for her handbag, her security bodyguard indicates tactfully that it is time to end the game with the baby and move on.

As she leaves, Raisa says to the nearby spectators that she is happy that her husband is so popular in East Germany, and she hopes that *glasnost* and *perestroika* will soon be established in their country and people will be free to travel. Only one person is unhappy: Erwin, the factory worker. He was prevented by security from getting near Raisa, but he hopes that with the advent of *glasnost* and *perestroika* he might meet her on her next visit.

When you look at the development of Raisa as a public figure on her overseas journeys, you realize how much she has learnt. She has greatly improved her English and understands fully what is said, and she has acquired the art of using the media to her own advantage and the trick of smiling to order. My own feeling is that Raisa will not become a conformist but remain an individualist, who, with her husband, Mikhail, will always be open to new experiences. I believe that nothing better could have happened for Russia than to have obtained the positive public relations skills of Raisa.

The world has through the media been able to observe how the wife of a Soviet party official, a lecturer in philosophy, has developed into a woman moving confidently on the international stage. In her own style, and using her own methods, she has conquered part of the world public. She smiles and scolds, she explains, makes charming gestures with her hands, and touches lightly but quite deliberately people standing close to her. She knows how to establish rapport with the international media, accepting and enduring their sometimes over-zealous attention. I believe she has ensured her place in history as the wife of the Soviet President who sought international peace.

Index